The Biblical God Doesn't Exist
Argument & Evidence

By John D. Espinoza

ISBN-13: 978-1492773290
ISBN-10: 1492773298

~~*~~

Table of Contents

Preface

How to use this book

What is an atheist?

Part I – Argument

1. Argument vs. Evidence

2. Rationality eludes us

3. Prove that it isn't

4. Something from Nothing

5. A finely tuned argument

6. Flawed by design

7. Are science and faith compatible?

8. Can they all be correct?

9. The fallacy of certainty

10. What you must accept to be a believer

11. The origins of god(s)

12. The probability of god

13. The Bible is the claim, not the evidence

14. Quoting from the Bible

15. Saul of Tarsus: Author of Christianity

16. The Nicene Creed

17. The Resurrection Myth

18. Was the Trinity a plagiarism?

19. It's just a theory

20. Does evolution disprove Christianity?

21. Put theology to the test

22. The Power of Prayer

23. Jesus and the Giant Game of Telephone

24. The Teachings of Jesus

25. Where was God?

Part II – Evidence

1. Absence of Evidence

2. The Great Flood of Noah

3. The twin cities of Sodom & Gomorrah

4. The Exodus

5. God on Trial

6. The Wrap

Appendix

About the Author

~~*~~

Preface

Raised in the Roman Catholic faith, I spent much of my early life in fear. Not the fear you may experience from the threat of physical harm, but more like the unsettled anguish one feels when they think they're in trouble. I attended the now defunct Holy Trinity Catholic School in New Jersey, which included church services each morning before class, and of course one had to put in an appearance on The Lord's Day. Six days of Catholic mass each week, regular confessions and nuns for teachers should serve to illustrate my young educational life.

My most vivid memories include being punched in the nose by a nun for having the audacity to chew gum during the Mass, and yet still proceed to receive The Body of Christ. Sister Theckla was the attacker on that memorable morning and none of my classmates were a bit surprised as she had a well-deserved reputation for physical torment of her students. My younger sister spent much of her time under Theckla's reign suffering from early morning diarrhea and actually pulled all of her eyelashes out one by one. Somehow, my mother never considered Catholicism could be the culprit for her rather significant nervousness.

When I was in the fifth grade, some of us boys would go across the street during lunch and clean up around the convent for the nuns. The main reason we agreed to do this was for the frogs. For reasons I cannot fathom today, I was quite a fan of frogs and toads and one particular spring day, I caught a large bullfrog and named him Ralph. I placed Ralph in a shoebox one of my peers found in the trashcan and took him back to class with me to await the end of the school day. Sister Noel was in a particularly foul mood that afternoon and was busy scolding us for not paying attention to her as she tried to instruct us. I picked this inopportune time to peer under the lid of my frog-filled shoebox to check on Ralph's status. When I looked back up, Sister Noel was coming down the aisle toward me with a full head of steam built up. She picked up the shoebox and held it high above her head, her arm fully extended. She peered down at me through her spectacles and then, with all the energy and force she could muster, threw the shoebox to the floor at my feet. "I dare you to pick it up," she sneered. A fool I was not. I didn't retrieve the box until class was dismissed for the day. When I finally got outside, I opened the box to check on Ralph and he was dead. The cause of death: Blunt Force Catholic Trauma.

Sister Leona was a gray-haired woman who kept a folded handkerchief under her watchband on her wrist. She frequently explained to her 8th grade class that this was a handy way to always be prepared for a sneeze. To my knowledge, none of my classmates followed her lead on that score. One fine morning, she was explaining how the girls in class were putting the boys in harm's way by hiking up their uniform skirts to show their legs. I was a late bloomer when it came to attraction to the opposite sex. In the 8th grade, I was still playing with GI Joes, so her speech was lost on me. I had difficulty understanding how a girl's legs could cause me any trouble, so I glanced over at Diana Perez and she had her tanned legs crossed under her desk and I did take notice that her skirt was very short. I remember feeling a sudden surge of embarrassment for her, as I was certain her underwear might show and then I looked back at Sister Leona, who was wrapping up her speech of doom and gloom. She had caught me checking out Ms. Perez's legs and told me in no uncertain terms that I was destined for an eternity on a fiery lake of burning sulfur. That was my first inkling that something here wasn't quite right, as the punishment just didn't seem to fit the crime.

I left Catholic School after 8th grade and attended a public high school in Long Island, NY. I never returned to the faith formally, but instead became what is commonly known as a lapsed Catholic. While I had doubts about what I'd been taught, I still believed in God and that Jesus Christ was the Son of God and that Heaven and Hell were real places. I didn't have the tools to deal with my doubts — that being the non-internet era — and I just generally avoided the topic whenever it came up. Becoming a parent changed that a bit.

While we decided to essentially raise our children without religion, my wife was Jewish by birth (which always struck me as odd that one is automatically Jewish because their mother is) and made one attempt to introduce my children to Judaism. My oldest daughter protested most loudly, as her education into Judaism seemed to include a significant amount of Holocaust coverage, which is bound to depress a young girl. The effort couldn't be sustained and we returned to our secular ways. I did manage to take a few lessons in reading and writing Hebrew though.

Years later, I received a text from my oldest daughter asking me what a "New Atheist" was. My initial reaction was to text back that there was nothing new about atheism, but since she was a freshman in college and taking a Comparative Religion class, I assumed her question was of a serious nature so I did what any dad would do when faced with such a thing: I turned to Google. What I found was truly astounding. Here were learned men, men of stature in their given professions speaking out openly against religion. I read everything I could about The Four Horsemen and felt something welling up inside of me. I ordered The God Delusion and as I started to read the preface, I felt that Dawkins had written the book specifically for me. Thus began the exciting liberation of my mind from the years of superstition into which I had been indoctrinated.

What you will find in this book is the culmination of the last few years of self-study, which may have started out as a quest for answers to the lingering questions from my religious youth, but has become instead a celebration of thinking and of reason and logic. I may have started out by reading the books of Dawkins, Hitchens, Harris and Dennett, but that was merely the opening volley. I've read voraciously since and watched countless debates and talks and presentations. I've attended lectures and engaged in minor debates myself. The process has been and continues to be exhilarating, and it has become more and more difficult to try to recall those feelings of fear and dread that were instilled in me by priests, nuns and others who possessed the "fear of God." Today, it all feels as flimsy as paper mache.

~~*~~

How to Use this Book

While I can make various arguments for the harm that religion does in the world, and the dangers represented by a faith mentality, the primary issue that I remain passionate about is that religion is false. The underlying premise is untrue, which means that everything that is built upon that premise is also untrue. The staggering amount of time, money, emotional energy and bloodshed expended in the name of something completely fictitious is a crime against humanity. So while there are debates about religion's place in society, whether the charitable works they do add value, whether they should have tax exemptions and access to power in government, whether the comfort some people seem to derive from their faith is worthwhile and should be left unchallenged, I will focus on one thing: To show that the God of Abraham, from which the three great monotheisms were spawned, does not exist.

7

I have read many books on the subject of gods, religions and belief in the supernatural. I've watched many debates on the matter as well, and one particularly vexing issue comes up frequently and leaves me feeling dissatisfied. That issue is the one of disproving the existence of God. Scientists will often stop well short of even making a claim about the existence of God, answering instead that one cannot prove a negative, i.e. we cannot prove that God doesn't exist. Many debates about the existence of God are often mired down in that esoteric point and the natural progression from there to debates regarding who carries the burden of proof. Arguments are presented and then countered and in the end, people must decide for themselves if they heard anything that impacted their thinking on the subject.

I began to think that I could build a compelling argument for the non-existence of God, but I wanted more than just arguments: I wanted proof. What you will find in this book is a combination of both. Part I features arguments supporting my statement that the god of monotheism; the God of Jews, Christians and Muslims featured prominently in the Holy Bible and the Quran, does not actually exist. In Part II of the book, I will use evidence, or more precisely, the lack of evidence where evidence should exist, to show beyond a reasonable doubt that the Biblical God is a mythical figure no more real than Zeus, the King of Gods from Greek Mythology. But before we start our journey together, I will state plainly that I am an atheist, which you probably figured out by now.

~~*~~

What is an atheist?

Atheists are among the most distrusted people in America and rank basically as unelectable to public office based on recent polling. When the American Atheists sued over a cross being proposed as part of a memorial to the World Trade Center in NYC–because it promotes Christianity, which is unconstitutional–a FOX News Facebook page featured hundreds of hateful, angry, violent and threatening comments against atheists in general, not just the group filing the lawsuit.

I don't wish to discuss the constitutionality of installing a cross on a memorial but I will mention that *anyone* could object to the legality of officially promoting one religion over another or promoting religion at all if the government is doing it. The US Constitution is pretty clear on that issue. This just happened to be the American Atheists doing the objecting.

I have encountered a lot of confusion regarding what atheism is, both personally and in what I've read on various blogs, social media and comments on websites where the topic is featured. Some suggest that atheism is actually a religion or faith-based belief system. So there seems to be a need to clarify just what an atheist is, and what an atheist isn't. Perhaps using a word that is less emotionally charged to explain myself will be beneficial. Let's take the word "typical." As defined by the Encarta Dictionary: English (North America), typical means representative or characteristic, having all or most of the characteristics shared by others of the same kind. Now we'll look at the word "atypical." It means, *not* conforming to the usual type or the expected pattern. In other words, atypical means not typical.

Now we'll look at the word "theist." A theist is a person with a belief in God, or multiple gods. There are monotheists, who believe in one god and polytheists who believe in many. Jews, Muslims and Christians are monotheists, believing in the God of the Bible. Many of the ancient religions were polytheistic like the Greek, Roman and Germanic or Slavic religions. Now, let's look at the word "atheist." As you might expect, an atheist is someone who does not believe in God or gods. In other words, atheist means not a theist.

That's really it. The atheist is not a theist, just like the atypical is not typical. It isn't any more involved than that, nor does it have any other meaning. There is no doctrine or dogma of atheism, no rules to follow or leaders who dictate what atheists believe. If you wanted to get really technical, there are some who further define atheism into segments like strong atheism and weak atheism, but I don't think that's a necessary distinction for the point I'm trying to make. If you want to know why someone is an atheist, there are likely as many reasons as there are people, but generally it's because the atheist has looked at the theist position, i.e. that there is a God or gods, and found insufficient evidence to accept that the position is true. That's certainly what it is for me. I've neither seen any compelling evidence nor does it make much sense to me logically. Everything I've learned and continue to learn about the universe and everything in it seems to me exactly how it would be if there were no God or gods.

Some atheists are opposed to religion just as some people are opposed to abortion or war, taxes or the Designated Hitter or the way some religious people are opposed to religions other than their own. But not all atheists are opposed to religion. Many don't give religion much thought, as it's just not a part of their lives. So if you find yourself in a discussion with an atheist who holds religion in disdain or contempt, you may certainly argue that point with that particular person but should refrain from assuming all atheists are the same, just as you wouldn't assume it of someone making an argument for or against any other issue.

I've purposely left out the agnostic so as not confuse the main issue but also because I've not seen the confusion with, and certainly not the anger that is directed at one who claims to be agnostic. I hope my attempt to define and clarify the word atheist will help at least remove some of the misconceptions. I can't do much about the trust issue though.

Before we move on, I feel that I need to say a few words about blasphemy because the rest of the book will feature content that by most definitions would be considered blasphemous. I find the concept of blasphemy deeply disturbing. Religions have created a protection scheme to keep their ideas from being questioned. Written into the so-called holy texts is a death sentence for even speaking irreverently about the god the author(s) created. These death sentences were carried out for centuries by the church and in many parts of the world today, 350 years after The Enlightenment, death is still handed out for speaking out. I am not referring to the lunatic fringe of one religion or another that would seek to commit violence against blasphemers, but actual governments of nations that convict and punish the act of questioning.

Imagine if you can, an idea for which it is a crime punishable by death for even questioning the legitimacy of the idea. One's ideas must be quite frail if a protection scheme is needed to guard them. Those of us who give credence to this protection scheme of archaic ideas, however dear they may be to some, are complicit in preserving it. I'm free to believe in leprechauns, fairies and pixies, but I have no right to have my beliefs protected from questioning or ridicule. You can believe that a god spoke telepathically to goat herders in Bronze Age Palestine, but you can't stop me from doubting it. Even inventing a punishment that is everlasting, doled out after death of course, isn't enough to keep someone from thinking if they choose to.

Just questioning the beliefs themselves is no longer enough. We must dismantle the prospect that any idea is safe from critical review, honest evaluation and intellectual questioning. No ideas are sacred and surely threatening violence and death for speaking about someone's ideas should be considered by all a crime against humanity and should be dealt with accordingly.

~~*~~

Part I - Argument

1. Argument vs. Evidence

There's a reason that human beings continue to argue about the existence of God. If God's existence were obvious, there'd be no argument. We'd all know He exists and is active in our lives and all this bickering, arguing, torturing and killing wouldn't be occurring. The reason it's still a question is evidence, or more precisely, the lack thereof. There's evidence and there's argument. These are two very different things and I'll make a layman's comparison of the two and explain why, on the evidence, God's existence is not obvious in the least.

One of the oldest arguments for the existence of gods is called the Argument from Ignorance. Take virtually any aspect of our natural world that we don't fully understand and you'll find someone claiming God is the answer, however as our knowledge of the natural world has increased, the pockets where God can be used as the explanation has grown exponentially smaller. But many people are ignorant of scientific explanations for things--even basic natural events like earthquakes or violent weather--and continue to point to God as the cause. Is this evidence of God? No, it is not. It is an argument for God and there's a difference.

Evidence is something that anyone can look at, and with the proper skills investigate and evaluate the information, and come to the same conclusions. It's a basic tenet of science and scientific inquiry. A scientist proposes an idea as to why something occurs and then goes about collecting data and analyzing that data to determine if it confirms his proposal; his hypothesis. If it does, he can now claim to know why that something occurs and present it to others to review. This is a key point. Others will review the hypothesis, the data and the results and should get the same answer. That would make the evidence fairly compelling as to the cause of the occurrence in question. Let's take our earthquake or weather event as an example. Someone claims it is an Act of God but collects no data, does no analysis and presents no findings. How would someone else then take this person's claim and verify it? They can't. Someone else claims that a shifting in the tectonic plates along a fault line between the two plates caused the earthquake. This can be tested, retested, verified and confirmed. In fact, it can be tested in various ways using various instruments, observations and tests and then reviewed by others until at last; we can say, "Yes, this is how the earthquake occurred."

Some people will point to a majestic and breathtaking feature of our natural world like the Grand Canyon and see God's handiwork. However, we know how the Grand Canyon formed and it wasn't via magic. If you aren't familiar with the formation of this astonishing hole in the ground, you really owe it to yourself to read up on it. It's awe-inspiring. So being ignorant of some natural event and pointing to God as the cause isn't a solid argument for the existence of God, but it is a convincing demonstration of your ignorance of the cause or origin of the event.

Others will argue that human consciousness and altruism, as well as our ability to know right from wrong are evidence that an Intelligent Being implanted our brains with this ability. While we do not know everything about the methods in which our brains function, we learn more every day and to date, have found no evidence to suggest we were magically programmed with a sense of humor, irony and the powers of cognition by a supernatural god.

Then there's the Argument from Design, which goes something like this:

- Every creation requires a creator. The more dramatic or complex the creation, the more likely this is evidence of some supernatural designer.

You'll hear things like, "have you ever seen a painting that didn't have a painter, or a house that didn't have a builder?" Again, this is merely an argument for a god, not evidence of a god. I can look at a pretty flower, or a snail's shell, or the human eye and say that God beautifully designed them. But someone else may look at the same things, create a hypothesis as to how they came to be, begin collecting data and testing their ideas until they come up with an answer which can then be verified by others using the same data and tests. The argument that God magically made the human eye is only compelling to those who would accept it at face value. There's no verifiable evidence to back it up and once you've seen the evidence and understand how the human eye came to be, the argument that a god did it becomes much less compelling. In a few chapters, we'll take a closer look at the apparent design in our world.

So it's important to understand the difference between making an argument for a god--and there are some complex and seemingly convincing arguments out there--and presenting verifiable evidence for a god. If there were verifiable evidence available, this would be a done deal. We'd all accept being God's little creations living to praise him and sing Hosanna all day and night. But the arguments for a god are only compelling to those who are willing to accept the arguments without looking into them further. I encourage you to shun these supernatural answers to your questions and keep an open mind as we continue down this steady course. We will expand our minds, pump some neurons and become enlightened and informed. It's a remarkably liberating, exciting and beautiful experience.

Challenge question:

If you're a believer in the supernatural realm of gods and spirits, I challenge you to grab a pen and paper and present your evidence for the precise location of the human soul, heaven and hell. No arguments please, just verifiable evidence that you can then present to someone else to look up, test and come to the same conclusions as you did.

~~*~~

2. Rationality eludes us

We are fortunate to live in an age of unfettered access to information on all manner of subjects, but the key to unleashing the full power of this access is to learn *how* to think about it all. Reasoned, rational, logical thought processes, applied critically and skeptically while looking at evidence is a goal we should all set for ourselves. Unfortunately, that just isn't the case for many people. Take for example, the reactions to a presentation on evolution at Appalachian State University given by evolutionary biologist and author of one of my favorite books on evolution, Jerry Coyne. These were a few of the comments posted on the ASU Facebook page:

- Never been less proud to be a graduate of App State...shame on you!

- It's a sad day when ASU would allow that foolishness to be taught. There are no facts for evolution because it is FICTION. Psalm 14:1 "The fool hath said in his heart, There is no God," I know there is a God. I am proof of that. Why don't you have one of your alumni come and talk on "The facts on how I know there is a God."

- Just look at the complexity of the human body. You can't just tell me that it just happened to come together. There must be a designed *[sic]*. There is a designer. His name is God.

- I wouldn't waste my time to read his book. You know why? Because I read The Book. It's called the Bible. Romans 3:4 "let God be true. But every man a liar"

- There are absolutely no facts for evolution! There are recreations and hypotheses for what scientists believe! There is more evidence the Earth is younger than people think than older! Also for Christians speaking up that believe in evolution, you need to check yourself! You either believe in the entire Bible or none of it. Genesis was not fiction so if you profess Christ you really are not professing him because without Genesis and sin, there would be no need for Christ!!

- This is a shame...what about a speaker on the Truth of Creationism? Equal time???

- I think it takes MORE faith to believe in Evolution. Although there is truth weaved within the theories, there is so much all of us are yet to understand.

We will visit many of these comments over the course of the book because they make excellent springboards to the points I wish to make, however suffice it to say for now that to refute evolution in 2013 is equivalent to refuting plate tectonics or gravity, or the germ theory of disease. It makes you look foolish and willfully ignorant. So how can it be that so many people, particularly in the United States and Turkey, refuse to accept the fact that life evolves? The single largest reason is religion, and with it the belief that a deity created all life in its present form, presumably through magic or the sheer power of its imagination. Poof: there's a platypus. But it isn't just scientific knowledge that people tend to refute; it's anything that goes counter to what they choose to believe. If the belief is deeply held, even cold, hard factual slaps in the face aren't going to jar the person loose from their preconceived beliefs. No human being is immune from this, although it is possible to train oneself to think critically, which helps break free the rooted trees of ignorance and misinformation that were seeded in our brains throughout our lives.

The human psyche is prone to innate biases that prevent us from being rational. Social psychologists have identified over a dozen cognitive issues that lead us astray and cause us to make serious errors in judgment. I think that being aware of them and learning how to recognize them is a major step in unwinding the muddled and tangled way we can sometimes approach information that feels unpleasant or uncomfortable. See if you recognize these biases and consider how they may keep you grasping tightly to ideas or beliefs that may be false.

Confirmation Bias: Our tendency is to agree with people who agree with us. We love to read or hear things that confirm what we already believe to be true. We are made uncomfortable by views and opinions that run counter to our thinking and it is this kind of preferential thinking that may cause us to hold onto certain ideas and opinions even in the face of contradictory evidence.

In-group bias: A throwback to our tribal roots, we innately trust and believe people in our in-group, while being fearful, suspicious and possibly even disdainful of other people. This bias prevents us from learning from people outside our small circle of trusted allies, who may not be the best sources of information.

Gambler's Fallacy: We erroneously put weight on past events to predict future ones. It's like thinking a baseball hitter "is due" for a hit because he's been hitless in the game thus far. The reality is that his odds of getting a hit are the same in his fourth at bat as they were in his first. If you flip a coin ten times and it comes up tails ten times, you may think heads just has to come up next, but the odds are precisely 50/50 on the eleventh toss too.

Post-Purchase rationalization: We use this bias to avoid feeling bad about something we bought after the fact. We convince ourselves that it was a really great deal or that we really needed it. We don't want to face the fact that we made a lousy decision. This ability to rationalize a bad decision helps us prevent cognitive dissonance, which is a very uncomfortable state of mind.

Neglecting probabilities: The easiest example of this bias is the widespread nervousness associated with flying. While the statistics clearly show flying is significantly safer than driving, our comfort with driving makes us choose incorrectly. We worry about being harmed or possibly killed in an act of terrorism, yet we are exponentially more likely to be accidentally harmed in our own homes.

Status quo bias: We tend to be apprehensive of change, which sometimes causes us to make choices and decisions that will keep things the same, or at least be the least disruptive.

Negativity bias: Bad news has a way of captivating us more than good news. We tend to think negative information is more important or profound and this likely has evolutionary roots. Being cautious and even paranoid would have helped our ancestors survive a much more hostile world than we inhabit today.

Bandwagon effect: We love to go with the flow of the crowd and we feel safety in numbers. A groupthink mentality can cause us to hold ideas that are very popular, but possibly not true. It's a part of our desire to fit in and be a part of a group. You may be familiar with the saying, "a billion Chinese can't be wrong," but they absolutely can be.

These are just a few of the most recognized biases, but social scientists and psychologists have repeatedly observed something they call "motivated reasoning." It's not that we don't want to be right or accurate, because we do, but the motivation is for us to arrive at a desired conclusion based on our own inherent biases. There is considerable evidence that we are more likely to arrive at conclusions that *we want to arrive at*, and we have the ability to construct seemingly reasonable justifications for these conclusions. In experiments conducted around issues like the death penalty, affirmative action and gun control, participants were given fake scientific studies, one supporting the impact of the aforementioned policies and one undermining their effectiveness. In each case, the participants felt the study most closely aligned with their own view was more "convincing."

In other studies, people rejected valid scientific data because the conclusions contradicted what they felt was true. Even providing additional evidence and argument didn't sway people; in fact they dug deeper. The best way to think of this phenomenon is that when we initially hear or read something that runs counter to our view of the truth, our initial response is an emotional one, like a fight or flight response. We begin to build rationalizations around our beliefs and dig in our heels on our positions. The cognitive and reasoning response from our brains is much slower, and in time, we may revisit the information and be able to break down our protective barriers and accept new information, discarding the old erroneous views. Or we may not.

~~*~~

3. Prove that it isn't

There are facts and there are opinions, there are truths and there are speculations. How do we separate them and know what is real and what isn't? Where does the burden of proof lie?

In the United States if a person is charged with a crime, that person is presumed innocent of said crime. He or she is under no legal obligation to prove his or her innocence. The burden of proof lies squarely with the person or persons accusing them of this crime. They must prove beyond a reasonable doubt that the person is guilty of the crime.

"The presumption of innocence (the principle that one is considered innocent until proven guilty) is a legal right of the accused in a criminal trial, recognized in many nations. The burden of proof is thus on the prosecution, which has to collect and present enough compelling evidence to convince the trier of fact, who is restrained and ordered by law to consider only actual evidence and testimony that is legally admissible, and in most cases lawfully obtained, that the accused is guilty beyond a reasonable doubt. In case of remaining doubts, the accused is to be acquitted. This presumption is seen to stem from the Latin legal principle that ei incumbit probatio qui dicit, non qui negat (the burden of proof rests on who asserts, not on who denies)."

So in a criminal proceeding we have our answer; the burden of proof lies with he or she who asserts.

If someone negligently causes damage to another, the injured party has a legal cause of action against the negligent party for compensation for damages caused. It's called a tort action and there are various rules and procedures that cover the process. I am concerned with one: where does the burden lie to prove both the damage caused, and the negligent act that led to those damages.

"Through civil litigation, if an injured person proves that another person acted negligently to cause his injury, he can recover damages to compensate for his harm. Proving a case for negligence can potentially entitle the injured plaintiff to compensation for harm to their body, property, mental well-being, financial status, or intimate relationships. Resulting damages must be proven in order to recover compensation in a negligence action, but each element of the case must also be proven. If the plaintiff proves only four of five elements for example, the plaintiff has not succeeded in making out his claim."

Again we see that the burden of proof lies with the party making the claim. They must not only prove their damages, but also prove each element of their case against the allegedly negligent party. They must prove for example that the party had a Duty of Care in whatever action they were doing that led to the incident. They must prove the party Breached that Duty. They must prove that said Breach was the Proximate Cause of the damages and of course they must prove their damages as well. So again, as in the criminal case, the Burden of Proof lies with the person making the assertion, not the one who denies it.

In the field of science, where incredible discoveries are made on an almost daily basis, there are specific methods used to find the truth. As you can imagine, one can theorize or hypothesize anything, but proving it is another matter.

"The Scientific Method refers to a body of techniques for investigating phenomena, acquiring new knowledge, or correcting and integrating previous knowledge. To be termed scientific, a method of inquiry must be based on gathering observable, empirical and measurable evidence subject to specific principles of reasoning. A scientific method consists of the collection of data through observation and experimentation, and the formulation and testing of hypotheses."

The scientific method has an emphasis on seeking truth. As written by Ibn al-Haytham, one of the originators of the Scientific Method:

"Truth is sought for its own sake. And those who are engaged upon the quest for anything for its own sake are not interested in other things. Finding the truth is difficult, and the road to it is rough."

The Scientific Method is used to test a hypothesis, a proposed explanation for how something is. The scientist will look for repeatable experimental observations to support or contradict the hypothesis. The hypothesis is not accepted as truth until it can be proven as such.

Again we see the same pattern emerging; one of proof. Consistently we see that the person or persons making an assertion, whether it be in a criminal case, a civil case, or a scientific one, has the burden to prove what they say is true. In no situation does the denier have to prove something isn't so.

So in no way does someone who disputes the assertion that there is a God in control of the Universe and watching over our every thought and all our deeds have any burden to prove that it isn't the case. The denier is under no obligation to prove something doesn't exist. As described in every scenario above, when seeking truth the burden of proof lies with the person making the assertion. If you think about this logically, without emotion or the deeply ingrained belief system that is religion, it makes perfect sense. If I were to make the following statement: "Unicorns exist and they come in many colors," you might say, "I don't believe that's correct." I could then respond by saying "Can you prove that they don't? How about leprechauns, trolls, elves, vampires, werewolves, the Loch Ness Monster, Santa Claus, or the Tooth Fairy? Can you prove they don't exist?"

Two great thinkers have illustrated the burden of proof beautifully and I will summarize and paraphrase them for you here. Bertrand Russell once said that if he proposed that there was a teapot in orbit between the Earth and Mars, no one would be able to disprove his claim as long as he was careful to include that it was so small as to be invisible to even our most powerful telescopes. But the fact that his claim could not be disproven did not give him the right to insist everyone accept it as true. Carl Sagan proposed that he had a fire-breathing dragon in his garage and invited you to come see it. Upon looking into the garage, you failed to see the dragon, to which Sagan replied, "It is an invisible dragon." You then proposed putting flour on the floor of the garage to see the dragon's footprints, but Sagan countered that the dragon floated above the floor. When you proposed that an infrared sensor could be used to detect the fire emanating from the dragon's nostrils, Sagan replied that the fire is heatless. For every physical test you propose to demonstrate the dragon's existence, Sagan has a reason why it won't work. Does the inability to disprove his assertion about a fire-breathing dragon in his garage mean that the dragon exists?

It's vitally important that we accept the burden of our assertions before we move on in the book, and I say that because I'm making an assertion for which I will bear the responsibility of proof. I am asserting that God does not exist, therefore I must prove my statement if I wish for you to consider it as a candidate for the truth.

~~*~~

4. Something from Nothing

Why there is something rather than nothing is one of the oldest philosophical questions known to man. It is *the ultimate* existential question, and it has led many to propose that everything that exists has a cause, and therefore because the Universe exists, it must have had a cause, and that cause is God. The argument, often called the First Cause argument, has been around for hundreds of years and refuted for hundreds of years, but if you've always been taught that God exists and took it for granted that He did, you may have never pondered this matter.

On January 6, 2011, then Pope Benedict told the world that God's mind was the force behind the Big Bang, and that the Universe was the result of the wisdom and inexhaustible creativity of The Creator. This is fundamental to the something from nothing argument. Before we knew much about the world, it was easy to tell the multitudes that an omnipotent God "created the heavens and the earth. Now the earth was formless and empty, darkness was over the surface of the deep, and the Spirit of God was hovering over the waters. And God said, "Let there be light," and there was light." This seemed like a perfectly plausible explanation for many. But as mankind's knowledge advanced, the Biblical account of God creating Earth before the Sun and other stars was proven incorrect. The Big Bang presents a great opportunity to again say, "There, there is where God started the Universe."

The Something from Nothing argument isn't limited to the entire Universe. Believers in God will also use it as an argument for the creation of life on Earth, quoting the Bible in Genesis indicating that God made everything in six days. Now it's true that man has not yet solved the riddle of how the very first living things came into being. Not yet anyway. But there are plenty of workable hypotheses to test. Think about this: when massive stars die in the most powerful show of explosive force in the Universe, the heavy elements in the star, created through the intense nuclear fusion of hydrogen atoms, are sent hurling out into space in a Supernova. These elements are the very same elements that exist in every living thing on Earth.

The thing about the Something from Nothing argument that really makes me shake my head is that the religious apologist, and the average religious believer, has no problem visualizing a God that has always existed. This seems a disingenuous way around the very argument they are making that everything that exists must have a cause. A special exception to this argument is made for God, which is rather convenient to say the least. The other aspect of the argument that I find confounding is that if believers in God credit Him with the creation of all things, of the Universe itself, aren't they in fact suggesting that God created everything from nothing? It would seem the faithful do in fact believe that something can come from nothing.

I strongly suggest that you read *A Universe from Nothing* by Lawrence Krauss and watch his presentation on YouTube of the same name. He presents the current level of understanding regarding the origins of the universe and I found it a truly fascinating read, even though I struggle with physics. In essence, we cannot see the quantum level of activity in seemingly empty space, but it is not in fact empty. There is energy in this empty space, in this nothingness. Residual, small-density fluctuations in empty space would eventually become all the matter and structure in the universe. The energy of empty space in the presence of gravity is the reason there is something rather than nothing. Nothing is unstable. Empty space is a "boiling brew of virtual particles that pop in and out of existence in a time so short we cannot see them directly." An asymmetry of matter and anti-matter, even if it were only 1 part in a billion, would leave enough matter left over to account for everything we see in the universe today. In fact, 1 part in a billion is exactly what is called for because today there are roughly 1 billion photons in the cosmic microwave background for every proton in the universe. The photons are the remnants of the early matter-antimatter annihilations near the beginning of time.

"It is said that men may not be the dreams of the Gods, but rather that the Gods are the dreams of men." – Carl Sagan

~~*~~

5. A finely tuned argument

An argument used for the existence of God borrows from the discoveries of scientists and points to the immutable laws of physics and says, quite correctly, that if one of the laws were off by even a small amount, the Universe as we know it would not exist. God had his hands on the dials, and finely tuned the laws to allow us to have a livable Universe.

I am not a physicist by any means, so I'm not about to delve deep into formulas of quantum mechanics, energy conservation or the law of thermodynamics. But Dr. Victor Stenger is, and in his book *God: The Failed Hypothesis* he discusses the laws of physics at length. He summarizes that "according to our best cosmological understanding, our universe began with no structure or organization, designed or otherwise. It was a state of chaos." If we look at what we know of the Universe as lay people, and consider the concept of a designer god at the controls, I think we can see our way through this advanced cosmological physics model without a PhD.

When Edwin Hubble discovered other galaxies in 1924, it was only his first incredible find. He also discovered that the degree of "red shift" observed in the light spectrum from other galaxies increased in proportion to their distance from Earth. This relationship became known as Hubble's law, and helped establish that the universe is expanding. Galaxies are screaming away from each other in all directions. If you backtrack their trajectory you get to a smaller and smaller universe until you reach the point of the Big Bang. There's a lot of work continuing to be done on the Big Bang, specifically trying to figure out what the universe looked like before the Big Bang. Check out the Science Daily website for the projects and hypotheses that are being worked on. My point though is this; if the universe were being created and finely tuned for us by God, why would he do it in this way? Why would He not create a firmament in the skies, as the Bible indicates? Why would He create a vast universe of mostly empty space and not put any life on Earth until 10 billion years after the Big Bang?

Let's take a look at these laws of physics that God allegedly dialed in for us so we could live here on Earth and see what they actually are. Human beings, in very recent years geologically speaking, have developed the ability to understand what we observe about the natural world around us. As I mentioned earlier, Hubble discovered other galaxies less than 100 years ago. Let's look at Newton's "Three Laws of Motion." He used these three "laws" to describe the way he saw the motion of physical objects and systems. This is a key concept to understand. Newton observed the way nature worked, saw that it worked consistently in that way, and wrote it down. So the laws are merely mans' observations of the physical world around us. All the laws of physics that the apologists claim were finely tuned for us to precise degrees are just the way the universe unfolded and works. The "laws" were written down after the fact, to explain what the natural world was already doing. They were not created before time as a blueprint for the universe to follow. As for the claim that if one of the rules were to be changed, the universe would not appear as it is today, I agree. It would be quite miraculous if that occurred.

Let's take a look at this natural world, supposedly designed and fine tuned just for us. The universe is 13.72 billion years old, give or take a few hundred million years. The Sun is approximately 5 billion years old, and the Earth, somewhere around 4 billion years old. Homo sapiens (that's us) did not appear on Earth until somewhere around 200,000 years ago (let's not quibble over a few centuries please). That means that mankind has inhabited the Earth for less than .01% of its existence. The universe has spent almost its entire existence devoid of life. So has the Earth. There have been 5 Major Mass Extinction Events in Earth's history, the last one 65 million years ago when T-Rex and his buddies bit the dirt for good.

75% of the Earth's surface is covered by ocean, which of course is not a friendly terrain in which we can live. Half of the Earth's land mass is desert or high mountain ranges, which are not particularly friendly to us either. What I believe is one of the clearest arguments against fine-tuning for our existence is that the Earth can be a devastatingly unstable place. Volcanoes, earthquakes, tsunamis, hurricanes, tornadoes, mudslides, lightning strikes, droughts, heat waves and freezing temperatures plague mankind. Hardly what anyone could consider finely tuned.

Our sun throws most of its incredible energy off into space. Only a smidgen of it warms our planet. Ours is the only planet in our Solar System where we can live. The universe is so vast, that even traveling at the speed of light it would take us 4.3 years to reach the next closest star, Proxima Centauri, which is a red dwarf star with no known planets around it. The next closet star is 5.9 light years away, and the one after that, 7.7 light years. So as far as human beings are concerned, Earth is it. One planet in the entire vast universe, 3/4 covered in uninhabitable ocean, with natural events wreaking havoc on its human residents. I'd suggest at this point that considering the entire universe fine tuned for our lives here is looking like a rather weak argument.

We live on one small speck of a planet, orbiting around one small to medium-sized star, in one of 100's of billions of galaxies racing through space at 1.3 million miles per hour. To presume the entire universe is all about us is a fairly large and arrogant presumption, but to also propose that God, 13.72 billion years ago, finely tuned this chaotic yet glorious universe for our use, in light of everything we've just discussed, is incredibly, unbelievably naive.

~~*~~

6. Flawed by Design

When we talk about the likely existence of a god, we can be referring to any type of supernatural deity, not necessarily the Judeo-Christian-Islamic God of Abraham. My goal is to disprove the existence specifically of the Biblical God Yahweh, not all possible gods. I'll be specific when I'm referring to Yahweh.

A frequent argument for the likely existence of a supernatural deity that lives outside the laws of nature (hence the term supernatural) is that Life, the Universe and Everything is just too complex, too detailed, and too perfect to have happened by chance or through some kind of natural process. It had to have been designed by a designer, a creator. Some of the examples used are the human eye, some of the more intricate flowers that have breathtaking symmetrical design, etc. The proponents of the design argument will state that even Darwin, who proposed the basis for evolutionary theory through natural selection, was amazed by the human eye and couldn't see how nature did it. He knew that somehow nature did, but he wasn't sure of the mechanism for it. Religious apologists will jump on this as an argument for the existence of a creator.

One of the original design arguments goes something like this: If you were walking along in the woods and saw a watch on the ground, bent to pick it up, you'd see immediately that it had to have been designed. It's really not an argument, but more of an attempt to create the plausibility for a premise. That premise is that you can tell by just looking at a thing that some form of intelligence designed it.

How can a human eye, a flower, a solar system, a Universe have come about through natural processes? They are so complex; they must have been designed by an intelligent being. The being must exist outside of our natural law, that's why we can't see it or him or her. The being must have existed before time, or outside of time, so it or he or she could have created everything from the beginning. It sounds pretty compelling.

Let's consider a few things rationally and logically, using our power of critical thinking, to see which of these things makes logical and rational sense. The universe and everything in it is natural. So this being, this god, would exist outside of nature. This god, who lives outside of everything else we know, outside of our Universe, also lives outside of time or else is older than the Universe, or is no longer alive but was at the beginning of everything. I've never heard a single religious apologist even suggest that god could be dead, so let's throw that out. So either god is very old, older than the Universe, or god exists outside of time.

This god, who lives outside the physical and natural laws that we know, and outside of time or is ancient beyond our reasoning, also has the knowledge to create everything we see, including the things that we can't see, and has complete knowledge of the laws of physics, chemistry, biology and mathematics to put everything in motion as it is today.

This god can also create a multitude of life forms; millions of species of plant and animal, individual and independent from each other (this god even made 37,500 different species of spider).

We could go on, but I think the point's been made. The evidence presented by religious apologists to support the likely existence of god, or the God of the Bible specifically, is that Life, the Universe and Everything is just too complex to have happened through natural causes. The best explanation is that of a designer. This designer lives outside the laws of the Universe, outside time or is ancient beyond human imagination, has incredible powers of creation to include physics, chemistry, biology, mathematics, genetics and more. This god can create planets, stars, galaxies, Black Holes, gravity, and all of the cosmos. This god created every species of plant and animal on Earth, everything we know, the entire Universe and all of the wonders of the natural world from nothing. There were no raw materials to work with, there was void, and god created everything through the powers of incantation. "Let there be light," said the God of Abraham and there was light.

It's time to think logically now. Critically. We should be skeptical and follow evidence and logic, not believe without questioning. The religious apologist's argument that we've been outlining here is that a designer best explains the complexity of the natural world. I've outlined the attributes this designer, this creator, this god or God would have to have in order to create everything in the natural world. This god or God would be magnificent beyond our comprehension, possessing powers we cannot imagine, be so complex of a being that human language would fail to adequately describe it or him or her. This god or God would be the epitome of complexity. This God would, by the apologists' own argument need a designer! There is no way this incredible being; this magnificent powerful deity of awesome power and dimension could have come about by chance or through natural processes. God must have been created, designed by a being even more magnificent, more awesome, and more impossible to comprehend. That being certainly couldn't have come about by chance or through natural causes. It or he or she too must have been designed.

The design argument is fundamentally flawed, by design. As much as human beings want a simple answer to the ultimate question, it just isn't possible. The most brilliant minds in the world work on, and solve, small pieces of the puzzle every day. We've seen back to the early stages of our Universe through the most powerful telescope built by humanity. The natural Universe is full of wonder, full of amazement and full of opportunity for us to learn, expand our knowledge and rejoice in the wonder of us. A God isn't necessary in that equation. We don't need to have a supernatural deity to experience the incredible Universe we're privileged to be alive in. It is awe-inspiring enough in its natural state.

Here's a homework assignment for you. Read up on the human eye. You'll find that while it's perfectly functional, the "design" of it leaves no question that it was not intelligently designed at all. The retina is barely attached and can be easily detached; we are effectively night blind due to the shape and pattern of our rods and cones. We have a huge blind spot where the optical nerve connects to the brain. There is a lot more, but I don't want to do your homework assignment for you.

~~*~~

7. Are science and faith compatible?

An area that I find frequently disturbing is when scientists refuse to acknowledge or address the issue of faith when asked if it is compatible with a scientific worldview. It's as if the continued special treatment given believers in the supernatural have muted these men of evidence, observation and testing. In my view, the only reason to ask if science and faith are compatible is if you're looking to debate or argue just to make some points because faith in the supernatural is diametrically opposed to scientific thinking. Remember that science is a discipline in how to observe the natural world. It is more a method of thinking than anything else. Faith, by definition, is belief in the absence of evidence, where science, by definition, is the search for evidence to support a hypothesis or idea.

Science asks questions, looks for answers, and then keeps looking. Science says "I don't know" then sets out to seek the knowledge, always knowing full well it may not find it. Science sees the wonder, awe and magnificence in the miniscule probability of life and rejoices in it. Science shows us the incomprehensible majesty of what's beyond our sight. When science finds an answer, at least a probable one, it can't wait to share it with humanity. Like an excited child learning something for the first time, science leaps at the chance to amaze and instruct, often to an only mildly interested audience. Science stares bravely into the dark corners and turns on the lights. Science sees a need, and is determined to fill it for the betterment of all living creatures. Science says, "I was wrong" and doggedly returns to the fight, determined to find a better way to get better answers. Science doesn't discriminate. Science is happy to study the tiniest molecule or the entire Universe. Science is patient, science is tolerant and science loves surprises.

Faith believes. Faith believes it knows. Faith doesn't need additional information nor does it necessarily want it. Faith would like others to agree on faith alone. Faith will look in dark corners and create frightening beasts. Faith says, "what if you're wrong?" and leaves it at that. Faith tells its audience to believe in ancient texts, in superstitious words. Faith isn't interested in new information. Faith isn't fascinated, faith isn't curious, faith already knows. Faith would have one believe they live in the ultimate totalitarian regime, with an omniscient being who watches our every move and our every thought. Faith would have one believe they cannot escape this regime, even in death, as we are immortal. Faith needs no evidence to tell us this and faith will scoff at us for asking for evidence. "Take it on faith my friend, you can trust me." Faith discards evidence contrary to its belief. Faith never says, "I was wrong." Faith indoctrinates and manipulates, faith uses guilt as a weapon.

You tell me: are science and faith compatible?

8. Can they all be correct?

As we continue our search for the truth underlying the premise of belief in God, I propose a thinking experiment for you:

- How can a Hindu, a Jew, a Christian and a Muslim all be objectively correct simultaneously?

If two things are contradictory, one or both are wrong. It's really that simple. That's the nature of contradiction. So if the Hindu is correct and the Lord Brahma created the universe (or many universes) and the Lord Vishnu maintains it, then the Jew, Christian and Muslim are all wrong. They believe Yahweh, the God of the Holy Bible, created the universe and everything in it. That can't be objectively correct if the Lord Brahma had already created it.

If the Hindu is wrong and the Vedas and all the tales in them are nothing more than myth, then perhaps the Jew is correct. However, if he is, then the Christian and Muslim are both wrong. The Jews don't believe Jesus was the Son of God, a part of the Holy Trinity. In fact, they think this Trinity goes against the monotheistic concept of one god. So if the Jew is correct, the messiah is yet to come and the Christians and Muslims have picked the wrong men to follow. The Muslims believe Mohammed received the final word from God and if they are correct, the Jews are waiting in vain as the messiah is not coming. They believe Jesus Christ was a prophet, not the Son of God and in fact, find the concept of God fathering a child to be blasphemous. If Mohammed brought forth God's final revelation to mankind, the Christians have picked the wrong man in Jesus Christ to worship because he is not a divine part of the three-headed God of Christianity. Of course if the Christians are correct, the Jews missed the boat and Mohammed was mistaken in what he claims to have heard from God.

These four religions contradict each other in their deepest core beliefs. They simply cannot all be correct. Either Brahma created the universe or Yahweh did. It's possible that they both did in a collaborative effort, and perhaps that could be the start of a new religion, but neither the Hindu, Jewish, Christian or Muslim tenets support such a possibility. If Jesus Christ was the Son of God and currently sits in Heaven at the right hand of the Father, waiting to return to Earth to sit in Final Judgment, then the other faiths are wrong. They've missed the truth that only the Christians have identified.

Your thinking experiment is to consider whether the four religious people from my query can all be objectively correct simultaneously. The subtext to that thinking experiment is to consider whether all four religious people from my query can be objectively *incorrect* simultaneously.

9. The flawed thinking that is certainty

When it comes to religion, true believers are absolutely certain that their chosen religion is the correct one, while every other religion is incorrect. They may not consciously consider this, but a Christian does not think the Hindu or Buddhist is correct in their beliefs, or they wouldn't be Christians. To hold Hinduism and Christianity as both being true would create serious cognitive dissonance. Perhaps without knowing, the truly faithful have taken the incredibly arrogant position of certainty. With one book, or a small collection of them, they have staked their claim to know things that no human being could possibly know. They claim absolute knowledge not only of the beginnings of the universe and of all life, but they claim to know the mind of the creator of all that is seen and unseen, to know what the creator wants from us. No academic, no scientist for example, would make such an extraordinary claim of absolute knowledge even in their own field of expertise where they have spent a lifetime of study, experimentation and observation.

Consider how quickly and decisively a Christian, Muslim or Jew dismisses the Hindu gods as false, yet have complete certainty in their own god. In order to be one of the billions of believers in the God of Abraham, one must state with utter conviction that the ancient Sumerians were wrong, as were the Egyptians. Their gods were fabrications of men. Imaginary beings concocted by primitive people. The Chinese, who have the longest running civilization in human history, were and are still clearly deluded in their Buddhist beliefs. The Hittites, creators of iron weaponry in ancient Babylon, were also wrong, and apparently especially gullible as they thought all gods were legitimate. When they conquered another group of people, they took on their gods as well.

Think of how far astray the ancient Greeks were with their pantheon of gods. This highly advanced civilization who brought the world great advances in math, science and the arts, as well as some of the most famous philosophers in the history of humanity were just dead wrong when it came to the supernatural. Certainly Zeus, Odin, Poseidon, Hades and the entire pantheon of gods worshipped by millions were a figment of the imagination of those archaic thinkers.

Of course the Roman Empire, the most famous of the ancient civilizations, were also completely wrong when it came to gods. Though they were the most powerful civilization in the world in their heyday, they just couldn't get the supernatural quite right. The Mayans: wrong. Incas: wrong. Aztecs: wrong. The aforementioned Hindus, despite the fact that millions of them believe in the Lord Brahma, are also wrong.

But the ancient Hebrews living in the desert 3,000 years ago, they nailed it. Somehow the revelations that every other culture and civilization received from their gods were mistaken, but when someone wrote the tale of Abraham, being visited by Yahweh in the mountains–where the important cutting of the skin from penises was discussed–this revelation was indeed the holy word of our creator.

The average believer in the tale of Yahweh, who punished Adam for his sin against Him when he ate of the fruit of the Tree of Knowledge, cannot seem to see the similarity between these tales and any of the tales of Greek or Roman Mythology. Yahweh punished the progeny of Adam, causing man to be born in sin–Original Sin–until God sent himself to Earth–via a virgin of course–to be sacrificed as payment for the Original Sin that God had lovingly bestowed upon mankind in the first place. Only Christians believe this portion of the old tales found on parchment, written by unknown authors and filled with conflicting testimony. The Jews, original followers of Yahweh, still await the Messiah who will usher in the coming of Yahweh's kingdom on Earth. Muslims believe that a merchant, Mohammed, received the final word of Yahweh via revelation, which he then had written down for him as he recited the revelation, apparently from memory, and thus Yahweh ceased his official communication with mankind.

Choosing to believe any of these tales as factually accurate and embracing them as a means to form your worldview, to perhaps model your life around, is certainly within each person's prerogative. But to insist that your chosen belief is the absolute truth, that no more information is required or desired, and then to insist others believe so as well, upon pain of discrimination, threats, violence or even death is reprehensible.

A believer need only consider what evidence or basis they use to dismiss the mighty Thor, God of Thunder, wielder of the hammer Mjolnir, as being an imaginary creation of the Norsemen and use that same evidence or basis to assess their own god. The Christian, Jew or Muslim is almost as much of an atheist as I am for they don't believe in any of the thousands of gods inscribed upon ancient writing, scattered throughout the infancy of our species. The Hindu is an atheist when it comes to the God of Abraham, and the large majority of the world's people doubt the veracity of Scientology and their thetans.

To convince yourself of the certainty of your beliefs, without honest assessment of your position, is a surrender of the gift of cognitive thinking. To blindly go forth with your belief-dependent reality and confidently insist upon its absolute truth is an absurd level of arrogance. The only honest position is one of inquiry, one of curiosity, one of perpetual learning. It takes courage and strength of character to move outside of what may be a lifetime of beliefs (which is why I vehemently argue that children should not be taught the myths of a parent's chosen religion as if they were true). But the joy of discovery, the awe of understanding and the beauty of reality make the fallacy of certainty a dark and dreary place.

~~*~~

10. What you must accept to be a believer

To objectively look at the ancient belief system that is religion and come away still believing it to be a true view of the world we inhabit and its origins, or that it somehow represents revelation from the beyond, gifted to the author of the particular text, is difficult to understand. We have much better explanations now for the natural world, the universe as a whole, and for organic life. These are testable and falsifiable positions, continually refined as new information is discovered. The religions spawned from ancient texts and rituals read exactly as one would expect of ancient texts and rituals. Take Judaism as an example, the patriarch of monotheism that would later give birth to Christianity and Islam. Judaism is no more than 3,000 years old, which should already give one pause. Human beings have been on the earth for quite a bit longer than that, and if the Creator of the Universe revealed Himself to a man named Abraham in a desert mountain, the natural question to an objective observer would be, 'Why did He wait so long to appear to human beings?'

To accept the premise of Judaism as objectively true, one would have to accept that Abraham was truly visited by Yahweh, an invisible entity that apparently has unimaginable powers, and that what Abraham told everyone was truly divine communication, and not just something he imagined or made up. To go even further, one would have to accept that Abraham was even an actual person, and not one of legend. As Israel Finkelstein and Neil Silberman wrote in "*The Bible Unearthed*," there is no evidence that the Jewish Patriarch was a real person. Additionally, you'd have to accept that the authors of the relevant parchments accurately wrote what was transpiring in a time when the human knowledge of the world was at its infancy and that scribes accurately copied these parchments–whose original copies are nonexistent–over the centuries and that they were accurately translated in later centuries.

Consider that in Jewish tradition, God Himself gave the contents of the first five books of the Jewish Bible, The Torah, to Moses, who would compile all of this divine guidance and wisdom and write it down. Even if this actually took place, i.e. that a man named Moses wrote the five books of the Torah, you would have to accept that Moses accurately wrote down communication he received, apparently telepathically, from an entity that exists outside of time and space, that has the power to spin galaxies of billions of stars with just the power of His imagination. You'd also have to accept that the communication this unfathomable being provided to one lone human being in a Middle Eastern desert consisted mostly of dietary restrictions, sexual restrictions, instructions on animal sacrifice and direction to annihilate rival tribes and take their virgin girls. Remarkably, this man that Jewish tradition calls the greatest prophet, leader and teacher that Judaism has ever known, probably never existed.

Judaism as a religion today is a very loosely interpreted set of ideas, moving far from the original divine instruction provided by the one true God to Moses. One can actually believe in none of the Jewish faith positions and still call themselves a Jew. This is quite remarkable to consider if the words of the Torah were truly divine guidance. Modern Judaism can be boiled down to something as simple as belief in God and God's relationship with mankind. I've often wondered on what authority Jews can disregard God's quite specific direction, but in reality, it's nothing more than modernity creeping into tradition and superstition, myth and legend and people realizing it for what it is: old stories from Judaism's early days.

Christianity requires even more remarkable suspension of common sense and reason than Judaism, which is no small thing. Not only must you accept the tales of Judaism, but you also must accept that the Hebrew God impregnated a young woman in desert Palestine, seemingly against her will, and produced an offspring of God and human DNA. This young god-man would eventually begin preaching, performing various miracles like raising people from the dead, curing blindness and leprosy and feeding thousands with a few loaves of bread and a fish. This god-man would ultimately be arrested and convicted of some offense, tortured in the most heinous and cruel manner, and nailed to a cross by the Roman Empire where he would die, but fear not believers, for he would not stay dead. God's only son would rise again, escaping death's cold, eternal grip, and levitate from the confines of Earth's atmosphere to join the Hebrew God in a divine kingdom.

While this story is far-fetched enough to cause an objective reader to raise an eyebrow, what is even more sensational is the reason for the entire enterprise. Using the books of the Torah previously discussed, the creators of this new offshoot religion used the Fall of Man from God's good graces as the reason for Christ's life, torture and execution. God had punished all of mankind for wickedness and apparently felt the need to forgive the poor humans at some point, and rather than just forgiving them, He forged this elaborate plan. The Creator of the Universe now laid the path to forgiveness bare. All would be forgiven by simply accepting the god-man as your personal savior. This is a completely voluntary action on each human being's part, but a failure to take the proffered olive branch will result in an eternity of suffering and torture in a place called Hell.

Again consider the things you must accept for this to form an objectively true view of the world. You would have to accept the Hebrew God of course, since it is His DNA that would have been coursing through the veins of Jesus Christ. You would have to accept the Torah and the divine revelation to the legendary and mythical Moses. You would have to accept that Jesus Christ was an actual person, a historically true living being. And of course you would have to accept that he rose from the dead and flew away into an undetectable celestial kingdom. This is before we even begin to consider the rest of Christian doctrine.

- It's interesting to ponder that if Jesus Christ ascended bodily into Heaven as is taught in Christian theology, and is seated there today at the right hand of The Father, then Heaven must not be very far away. If Jesus had been traveling at the speed of light (186,000 miles per second) when he left the planet Earth, he'd still be traveling through the Milky Way galaxy, which is approximately 100,000 light years across.

The Gospels of the Christian Bible tell the story of Jesus of Nazareth and attempt to have him fulfill prophecy of the Jewish Bible so that he would be seen as the Son of God. These parchments were written decades after the alleged death of the man called Jesus and their true authorship is unknown. You would have to accept that these accounts accurately depict the life and times of Jesus, even though the authors had no first hand knowledge of the accounts. There are no original manuscripts, so you would have to also accept that the scribes who copied them by hand over the centuries did so accurately. What I perhaps find most fascinating is that the first recorded mention of the only son of the Creator of the Universe was written in the year 49 of the Common Era, a full 16 years after the death of God's progeny. No one alive during the time that God's son was walking the earth, performing feats that violated the laws of nature, bothered to mention any of it. The man who finally wrote the first words about Jesus Christ was a man named Saul, and he single handedly created much of what you have to believe if you are to consider yourself a Christian. Remarkably, Saul never knew or met Jesus Christ, but came to understand the Creator of the Universe's plans for mankind through a vision, a divine communication once again, that was so potent, it blinded him for three days.

If one were to objectively read the Gospels, without even knowing that they were written decades after the life and death of the supposed Jesus of Nazareth, one would find significant discrepancies. This alone should give the person of average intelligence, education and experience enough reason for consternation. How could the account of what would be the most important person to have ever lived and breathed be quite so faulty? With a bit more probing, one would find that leaders of the early Church selected these Gospels and that all other documents that could have been considered part of God's Word were destroyed. Unfortunately for the Church, more manuscripts have turned up over the years to cloud the picture they were trying to paint.

Lastly, in order to consider the Christian view of the world, its origins and its ultimate destiny to be true, one must believe that all human beings are immortal. This most basic belief, that humans have "souls" that live on beyond the death of the body, is required to be accepted in full for any of the Christian worldview to matter. A brief study of man's recorded history will show that every civilization in history has invented an afterlife, clearly displaying our inability to accept the finality of our demise. It wouldn't be much of a simplification to state that every religion ever invented sprang forth from our fear of death, our fear of not being. There isn't a single piece of evidence to support that there is an incorporeal essence in every person that is either independent of the body or able to leave the body and continue to exist. To be a Christian though, you must accept that this invisible, conscious and apparently undetectable essence exists and that it is this essence that God is interested in after your body dies.

Muslims consider Islam to be the one true religion. They too must accept the Hebrew God as a real entity, the actual Creator of the Universe. They too must accept that this invisible, unbelievably powerful entity that resides outside of time and space in an undetectable kingdom is interested in us, created us from a clot of blood, and has plans for us in this life and the next. Divine communication again takes center stage as Islam features the prophetic words of one man: the Prophet Muhammad. To accept Islam as truth, one must accept that the Prophet Muhammad received not only direct communication from God, but that said information was God's final communication to mankind. How does the objective enquirer know that Muhammad received telepathic guidance from The Almighty? Because Muhammad said he did. In fact, Muhammad reported continuing to receive Godly communication until his death. These communiqués from the beyond form the verses of the Quran around which Islam is based.

In order to accept that Islam is objectively true, one must also accept that the Creator of the Universe uses angels to deliver His divine messages. One of these, the Angel Gabriel, provided the final words of God to Muhammad. There is no evidence that such beings exist. You must also accept the previously discussed immortality of human beings through the incorporeal soul, and that the purpose of human existence is to worship God until the final Day of Judgment, when there will be bodily resurrection of the dead to face God's judgment of the manner in which your life was lived. Islam literally means submission to God.

The objective enquirer, now having taken in a brief overview of the three monotheisms that dominate much of religious society today, can step back and see a common thread. A thread so thin as to be invisible, yet without this thread there is no religion. That thread is revelation. To accept any of the three monotheisms as true (and since they cannot all be true, the more likely position is that neither of them are), one must be willing to accept revelation from the divine. It has always interested me to know how one chooses which revelation to be the real one. If Muhammad's revelation was true, Islam is the one true religion and all followers of Saul of Tarsus's revelations of Jesus have been duped. If Moses received the true revelation, then the Hebrew people are indeed God's chosen people. Did Saul of Tarsus receive the one true vision of God's only son and formulate the basis for man's only path to eternal bliss? If he did, then the Jews and Muslims, not to mention the other 67% of humanity that is not Christian, are seriously mistaken.

Thomas Paine was one of the Founding Fathers of the United States of America. Friend to Jefferson and Franklin, outspoken revolutionary and author, he wrote this of revelation in his epic demolition of the Bible, "The Age of Reason":

"No one will deny or dispute the power of the Almighty to make such a communication, if he pleases. But admitting, for the sake of a case, that something has been revealed to a certain person, and not revealed to any other person, it is revelation to that person only. When he tells it to a second person, a second to a third, a third to a fourth, and so on, it ceases to be a revelation to all those persons. It is revelation to the first person only, and hearsay to every other, and consequently they are not obliged to believe it.

It is a contradiction in terms and ideas, to call anything a revelation that comes to us at second-hand, either verbally or in writing. Revelation is necessarily limited to the first communication — after this, it is only an account of something which that person says was a revelation made to him; and though he may find himself obliged to believe it, it cannot be incumbent on me to believe it in the same manner; for it was not a revelation made to me, and I have only his word for it that it was made to him.

When Moses told the children of Israel that he received the two tables of the commandments from the hands of God, they were not obliged to believe him, because they had no other authority for it than his telling them so; and I have no other authority for it than some historian telling me so. The commandments carry no internal evidence of divinity with them; they contain some good moral precepts, such as any man qualified to be a lawgiver, or a legislator, could produce himself, without having recourse to supernatural intervention."

So finally, we come to what it truly takes to accept a religion as your worldview, as a true depiction of the origins of the cosmos and of life on our blue-green planet. I refer here not to the loosely weaved spiritualists of the modern era, who believe in personal relationships with a higher power of their own understanding, who feel a part of something more than the natural world. To address those kinds of belief systems, I'd have to literally take each one separately as the beliefs are wide and varied. I am also not referring to the Jews, Christians or Muslims who follow some of the traditions of their parents and grandparents and have celebratory dinners at certain times of the year because their families always have and it's a way to honor their culture and their history. I'm referring to the truly religious, the true believers in their chosen faiths, those who believe in their holy texts and the revealed Word of God.

It takes a willingness to believe. These systems of religious belief fly in the face of everything rational and reasonable about human knowledge. The characters are often mythical, the stories embellished, the themes borrowed from the religions of civilizations past. To accept any of the monotheisms as truth, one must literally close their minds to the advancements of our ancestors, who through relentless efforts have solved seemingly unsolvable mysteries, cured seemingly incurable diseases and brought us the wonders of the natural world in observable and testable ways. One must be willing to ignore the universe that we are discovering, which cares not for us at all, and instead believe that true knowledge was given to a select few men in the Bronze Age and that somehow this knowledge will "save" one from God's judgment. Believers will call it faith, but faith is nothing more than believing something to be true because you want it to be true, even though there is no good reason to do so. I fail to see how this can be considered virtuous as it is nothing more than wish-thinking and self aggrandized delusion that somehow, in spite of everything we know, the Universe really is all about us.

~~*~~

11. The origins of gods

As children we are taught that a man, an immortal man, lives in the North Pole with Elves. This immortal man knows if every boy and girl in the world has been good or bad, and he uses this information to determine if he will give him or her a toy. You see, he and his Elves build toys all year long and then on one special night, the immortal flies around the world in a sleigh drawn by magic flying reindeer and he delivers all his toys. That's right boys and girls, all in one night.

As children grow they start to see the impossibilities of this scenario and see through the illusion. It's a sad realization perhaps, but better a sad truth than a pretty lie. The age of innocence passes at that moment as tooth fairies, giant pink bunnies and other mythological creations lose their standing and become just another storybook tale. There is one such tale that children are told that lingers though. This tale somehow survives the end of innocence and embeds itself in the crevices of the grey matter in our skulls and for some, lasts a lifetime.

The oldest organized religion in the world is Hinduism, which dates back some 1,500 years before Christ. It has no known creator; it is more a melding of ideas over generations. However even before organizing into religion man has worshipped. Paganism or Earth worship is ancient, possibly as much as 30,000 years old. So what is it that compels human beings to create stories of powers greater than themselves, to create deities and other characters in dramas every bit as suspect as that of Santa Claus? It would seem that the quest for knowledge, especially the knowledge of creation, of where everything we see came from, of where we came from, is a question man must answer.

The Greeks created their gods to explain the world around them. The god Chaos was the foundation of all creation. From creation other gods came into being to rule the earth, the heavens, even emotions such as love. The Egyptians believed Amun created all things, but they too had many gods: Ra, the god of the sun, Sekhmet, the god of destruction and Geb, the god of Earth among them. In fact, creation myths permeate all cultures around the world. These stories all feature some form of creating the cosmos from a state of chaos or a state of nothingness. These myths feature characters and usually a deity or two. In Africa, where man first appeared on earth, there are many creation myths. Not surprisingly, there are many similarities:

- Earth was water & darkness ruled by the giant Mbombo. He vomited up the sun, moon and stars. He would vomit again later, throwing up some people, animals, and other such things as we see on earth.

- The early Kenyans believed the creator Enkai fashioned the origins of humanity.

- The people of Mali believe Mangala created everything by the use of various seeds.

- In Benin, there is Mawu, the creator. Mawu created everything as she rode on the back of a rainbow serpent. The earth was created first, and the winding motion of the rainbow serpent created hills and valleys while the serpent's excrement created mountains.

While these may seem like far-fetched stories to us today, consider the story of Genesis in the Judeo-Christian traditions. Creation of all things is done in six days by divine command of a nameless God. God created man out of dust and breathed life into him. God removed a rib from the man to create woman. The Mayans believed their gods, Tepeu and Gucamatz came together to make the world and they also created by divine thought. They had many false starts before finally making humans from maize-corn dough. The Incas creation theory is that the god Con Tiqui Viracocha emerged from a lake bringing some humans with him and then created the sun, moon and stars to light up the world.

There are many stories written by men that show the various gods interacting with humans and becoming very involved in their lives. One of the most fascinating to me has always been the virgin birth of Christ. I'll get into that more in a moment, but amazingly there have been lots of other stories of virgin births throughout history. Two thousand years before Christ the Egyptians told of a virgin birth when the god Taht advised the virgin Queen of Egypt that was she to be a mother. The god Kneph mystically impregnated the virgin.

- Horus was the child of his virgin mother, Isis.
- A ray of light begot Apis, a sacred bull.
- Ra, the sun god, was born of a virgin mother and had no father.
- Attis was born of Nana, who conceived him by putting an almond in her bosom.
- Dionysos, a Greek God, was miraculously begotten as well with an interesting twist. He was removed from his mother's womb before fully ready and implanted in Zeus' thigh to finish out his gestation.
- Jason, slain by Zeus, was a child of the virgin mother Persephone.

There are more of these virgin births, and lots of other stories of unusual births throughout history. Matthew and Luke tell us that the Holy Spirit provided the seed for Jesus Christ. How did they know? An angel told them. The reality is that when these men wrote these stories, similar stories had already been told for generations by the Egyptians, Persians and Greeks before them.

As man has advanced, remarkable progress has been made on the origin of species. We now know that the Earth, in its roughly 4.5 Billion year span, has been home to millions of species of plants and animals and that over 99% of them are extinct. Through DNA research we know that the chimpanzee is man's closest relative, with only a 2% variance in our basic DNA structure. Of all the Great Apes only man has 23 chromosomes vs. the chimp, gorilla and orangutan's 24. Human Chromosome 2 is a fused set of 2 chromosomes almost identical to 2 chimp chromosomes that are not fused together. We have also made incredible discoveries in space thanks to the Hubble Telescope. We have seen billions of galaxies, the light of which has been traveling billions of light years to reach the Hubble. It's an awe-inspiring thing to consider. Yet in spite of all we've learned and continue to learn, fables made and remade for countless generations of man continue to permeate the fabric of humanity on earth. Man is a remarkably curious species and for thousands of years has been trying to answer the same questions. The fact that some are so willing to believe these fables as facts, without the slightest evidence to support them, remains one of the most fascinating aspects of human behavior.

~~*~~

12. The probability of a god

As we've already discussed, the atheist generally doesn't accept the existence of a god because the evidence for a god isn't compelling. As promised, in the second half of the book I'm going to go beyond just not accepting the claims for a god, but make a claim myself: that one specific god, the God of the Holy Bible, doesn't actually exist. But for now, I'd like to go through a fun mental exercise with you around probabilities.

As we know, life on Earth is able to exist because we're just the right distance from our star; the Sun. Any closer, the planet's water would evaporate, and life on Earth needs water to survive and thrive, and it would be intensely hot. Any further and any water would freeze solid and it would be too cold to sustain life. Additionally, the Earth's orbit is elliptical, but it's not a particularly elongated ellipse so we're never too far out of that perfect zone.

The Milky Way, our beautiful home galaxy, is 100,000 light years across and has somewhere between 100 and 400 Billion stars in it. Astronomers have identified 921 planets around stars in the Milky Way so far, and if you extrapolate those numbers out over the billions of stars in our galaxy, there are likely billions of planets in the Milky Way.

There are hundreds of billions of galaxies in the Universe, many of them spiral galaxies like ours, but many are elliptical. Scientists have recently discovered that there are many more elliptical galaxies than once assumed and the elliptical galaxies have many more stars than the spirals. So with hundreds of billions of galaxies, each having hundreds of billions of stars, and many of those stars having planets, there are likely over a billion billion planets! That's a 1 with lots and lots of 0's after it.

1,000,000,000,000,000,000

These numbers are staggering and it's virtually impossible for our minds to actually comprehend figures of this size, but stay with me. Remember we're just talking about probability here; likelihood based on the data we have. So if there are that many planets orbiting that many stars, how many of those planets might be at roughly the same distance from their star that the Earth is from ours? Let's be very, very conservative and say just 1%. So 99% of all those planets are out of the "zone." That would give us somewhere around 10,000,000,000,000,000 planets that are in the habitable zone for the kind of life we have on Earth. Now let's assume that some of those planets have water on them, since they're at the right distance from their sun, and that they have all the heavy elements Earth has on them. If we use really astronomically bad odds that any kind of life has developed on these Earth-like planets, say 1 in 1,000,000,000 (one in a billion), there would be life on one million planets in the Universe.

You're probably saying to yourself, there's no way. That's too many assumptions, the data is extrapolated too far, the odds of getting these numbers even close to right is astronomically bad. I agree. So let's make it even more unlikely that there's life on any other planets. Let's take the number of likely planets and instead of predicting that 1% are in the habitable zone around their stars, we'll say only .01% are. We're taking the position now that the odds of any planet being the same distance from their star that Earth is from ours is ridiculously low. Okay, there'd still be 100,000,000,000,000 planets at the right distance. Now even if of those planets, which are at the right distance from their sun to have water, there were only a one in a billion chance that any life has developed on them, there would still be life on 1,000 planets.

Let's consider the exercise we've just gone through. Life is a wondrous thing. We've been unable to find any sign of life anywhere else but here on our home planet. And do we ever have life: millions of species of plants and animals living and breeding and making their way. It is so precious we have a difficult time imagining there could be life anywhere else. However, even using ridiculously bad odds of life existing anywhere in the Universe, we have to admit that it is at least probable that there is. And we're dealing with known, provable facts like galaxies, stars and planets.

Now imagine trying to calculate the probability that there exists only one entity that is somehow outside the laws of physics that govern our Universe. Not only is there only one, and this entity doesn't follow any of the laws of the Universe that the hundreds of billions of galaxies follow, but this entity has *always* existed. Not only is there only one, and this entity doesn't follow any of the laws of the Universe that the hundreds of billions of galaxies follow, and this entity has always existed, but also this entity created the Universe. Not only did this entity create the Universe, it created all of the millions of species of plants and animals we talked about earlier here on Earth. Not only did this entity accomplish all of this but this entity can read the minds of all 7 billion humans on Earth at the same time, hear the prayers of all 7 billion humans at the same time, and intervene in the events of the lives of these humans on Earth, all without ever having been seen or ever having left any physical evidence of its presence.

What is the probability, the likelihood that such a being, a god, could possibly exist? If it's hard for you to imagine that the Universe is teeming with life, with somewhere between 1,000 and 1,000,000 planets having life on them, how hard should it be for you to imagine that there's a god?

~~*~~

13. The Bible is the claim, not the evidence

The Bible is a collection of books that are considered sacred in Judaism or Christianity. There are many versions of the Bible, with different books appearing in different order. The Hebrew Bible contains twenty-four books divided into three parts: the five books of the Torah, the books of the prophets, and various writings. The first part of Christian Bibles is the Old Testament, which contains, at minimum, the twenty-four books of the Hebrew Bible divided into thirty-nine books and ordered differently than the Hebrew Bible. The second part is the New Testament, containing twenty-seven books: the four Canonical gospels, Acts of the Apostles, twenty-one Epistles or letters, and the Book of Revelation.

The oldest surviving complete Christian Bibles are Greek manuscripts from the 4th century. The Bible was divided into chapters in the 13th century and into verses in the 16th century.

It's important to understand that the Bible itself is not evidence of its own truth, but merely the information used by the religious for their worldview. In other words, the Bible is the claim. The religious claim that the Bible is true, and use it to claim that their doctrines are true. They claim that God divinely revealed the contents to men in the Bronze Age, and that its characters really lived the lives described, and that the events actually occurred. However, it is no more evidence of its veracity than the Lord of the Rings is evidence that hobbits and orcs exist.

In order to objectively prove that the Christian worldview is true for example, one could use the Bible as a starting point and begin to seek independent corroborative evidence that its tales are genuine. We can also attempt logical arguments that support that the doctrines are at least plausible and logically sound. Because the Bible is so large, with so many disparate books, we could just choose a few key elements of the doctrine and begin to collect the data necessary to prove our hypothesis:

- *The Christian worldview is true.*

A key element in Christianity is that Jesus Christ was the Son of God and died for our sins. This is a rather broad statement, but the various denominations have narrowed it down for us. For example, the Catholic Church states that, "*By his sin Adam, as the first man, lost the original holiness and justice he had received from God, not only for himself but for all humans. Adam and Eve transmitted to their descendants human nature wounded by their own first sin and hence deprived of original holiness and justice; this deprivation is called "original sin".*

So now we know what sin Jesus Christ died for, according to the Catholic Church. Methodists, Lutherans, Anglicans and Protestants all agree with this basic position. The Bible tells the tale of Adam and Eve and their sin against God, but that is not evidence of its occurrence, merely the claim on which Christians base their faith. To prove that it's true would require independent evidence of Adam's sin against God and the subsequent punishment, however such evidence would be impossible to obtain. The evidence shows us that humans evolved in Africa 200,000 years ago, descendant from other hominins, possibly directly from Homo Heidelbergensis, although we don't know that for certain. Could one of them have been the Adam who sinned against God? There's no way to know, so the physical evidence trail stops cold.

Could a logical argument be made for the claim of the Fall of Man? Christians claim that God is omniscient, which makes the logical argument for Christianity difficult. Since God is omniscient, he knew Adam and Eve would sin against Him and that they'd be punished by Him, and that ultimately He would choose to send His Son to Earth to give humans a chance to remove the sin that He had placed upon them in the first place. He knew all of this before it ever happened, which begs the question why He did any of it at all? It would seem to make human beings an experiment or a game God is playing, to see if future human beings would follow His lead through Jesus and find salvation. But of course, He'd know if we would or not because of His omniscience, and it leaves the awkward span of time before Jesus where none of those humans would have had the chance at redemption. It's a fairly illogical proposition, and would require many assumptions and speculations to try to resolve.

Another key component of Christianity is Christ's resurrection from the dead and ascension into Heaven. This tale is told in the Gospels, but that fact alone proves nothing. Did the resurrection happen? To test this hypothesis central to Christianity, we could attempt to look for contemporary reports of this seemingly impossible event, and we'd find that there are none. There is nothing in the records of the time confirming either the crucifixion of Jesus or his resurrection from the dead. We could look for physical evidence, but because the body of Christ ascended into Heaven, we can find no physical evidence. We could look for Heaven itself, but to date, even with the Hubble Telescope showing us the wonders of the early Universe, we've seen nothing that could be a celestial kingdom filled with souls. It's possible that Heaven is invisible to us, which makes it impossible to prove or disprove, and therefore our hypothesis of Christ's ascension is also impossible to prove or disprove.

So you can see with just these two examples how the Bible itself proves nothing. It tells a story, which would lead someone seeking the truth of it to collect data and test the hypothesis, derived from a reading of the Bible. Already we see that its first claim, that of the Fall of Man, cannot be proven independently to have occurred, nor does it make a sound logical argument as a premise. The resurrection of Jesus Christ also cannot be proven to have occurred, and of course logically, one cannot argue that resurrections from the dead are even possible.

So in our quest for truth about the existence of God, the Bible stands only as a basis for that claim, not the evidence for that claim. Just as the Vedas tell the story of the Hindu gods, and Sammy Hagar's book tells the story of his abduction by aliens, these are claims of events, not proof of them. We are free to believe Sammy's claims; just as we are free to believe those of the ancient Hebrews or the Hindus, but that doesn't mean that what we've chosen to believe is true.

14. Quoting from the Bible

As we've just discussed, the Bible is a collection of parchments, of varying age, written in multiple languages by anonymous authors about whom we know almost nothing. The books contradict each other, present tales of myth--some of which are quite ridiculous--and exaggerated or completely falsified histories of Bronze Age tribes. The fact that these books exist does not make them factually accurate or intellectually relevant. Occasionally some supporters of the Bible and the religions based upon it will acknowledge that the tales aren't literally true, but will argue instead that they are metaphorical in nature. The issue with playing the metaphor card is that an uphill battle is created to determine what is metaphor and what is literal. For example, if I were to claim that heaven and hell are metaphors for good and bad behavior, or for peaceful vs. tormented living, on what authority would you claim that I am wrong? How do you know that heaven and hell are literally real places, but that Jonah living in the belly of a whale for three days, or Methuselah living to be 1,000 years old is metaphor?

The early Church leaders assembled these miscellaneous documents and edited them as needed to suit their purposes. The five books of the Torah for example were written over centuries and assembled around 450 BCE. The claim is that God Himself revealed them to Moses, although on what evidence this claim is made is anyone's guess. So when one quotes from Genesis, Exodus, Leviticus, Numbers or Deuteronomy, they are actually quoting anonymous authors, from unknown origins, who had less knowledge about the world than an elementary school student has today. This should not fill anyone with confidence.

Unknown authors also wrote the Gospels of the New Testament that tell us of Jesus, the Son of God. The oldest of these booklets was named Mark by early Church leaders and was written around 70 years after the birth of Jesus. The author or authors were not witnesses to any of the events they wrote about, nor did they have any writings by Jesus himself to go by. The reason they had no writings from Jesus is because there are none. Jesus, if he ever actually lived, never wrote a single word. The other three Gospels were written after Mark and used Mark as a source, as many of Mark's passages are found in the other texts. There were plenty of other writings available to use for the New Testament if Church leaders wanted them, but they chose these four and destroyed the rest. None of these books possess historical information that can be attested to as true. They are tales of hearsay, told and retold over generations until someone wrote them down and they were later chosen to be part of the Bible. There are some lovely quotes in them, as you can find in literature throughout mankind's history, but using these quotes to make your claim for the supernatural, for knowing the mind of the Creator of the Universe, is an absurdity. You are essentially claiming to know things a human being cannot know, simply because something was written down in an old book that was written by Bronze Age men of unknown identity, education, background or motive.

My strongest recommendation is to actually read the Bible, then read the history of the Bible's origins, then read the *Age of Reason* by Thomas Paine and other books that point out the erroneous and fictitious elements of the Bible. Upon completing this, if you choose to continue arguing for the legitimacy of the Abrahamic religions, you won't quote the Bible or tell the Creation story or Noah's Ark story or the inspiring tale from Matthew of the resurrection of righteous men from their graves upon Jesus' death, who then took a stroll through the city to visit old friends. You'll want better arguments than that if you want them to be compelling in any way.

"You shall not make for yourself a carved image — any likeness of anything that is in heaven above, or that is in the earth beneath, or that is in the water under the earth; you shall not bow down to them nor serve them. For I, the LORD your God, am a jealous God, visiting the iniquity of the fathers upon the children to the third and fourth generations of those who hate Me, but showing mercy to thousands, to those who love Me and keep My commandments." ~ God

~~*~~

14. Saul of Tarsus: Author of Christianity

One of the things that have most amazed me during the course of my study on this topic is how flimsy and thin the gigantic monotheisms actually are. The premises on which they are based are recycled myths from other eras of mankind's time on Earth, and even a brief analysis of their origins leaves one agape at how little there is in terms of any factual basis. In this chapter, we'll look into the story of Saul of Tarsus, who can arguably be called the author of Christianity. Saul, who would later change his name to Paul, is also the man who gave us the first recorded mention of Jesus Christ. His writings, most of which are believed by scholars to be legitimately his work, predate the Gospels whose authors are unknown, and while the Gospels focus on the life, preaching and death of Jesus of Nazareth, Paul's writing delivers the ideology for those who would choose to follow the religion that would bear Christ's name.

Saul of Tarsus was a Jewish man born in the year 5 CE. He proclaimed himself a Hebrew from the line of the tribe of Benjamin, was raised in Jerusalem, and as a young man participated in the persecution of the early Jewish followers of Jesus Christ. Jews did not accept Jesus as the Messiah because he didn't meet any of the criteria to be the Messiah. The Messiah, according to Judaism, will be a great political leader, a direct descendant of the paternal line of King David. He will also be a great military leader and win battles for Israel, establishing a Torah-based kingdom in Israel (the Torah being the first five books of the Old Testament, which Jews believe were dictated to Moses by God). Clearly, Jesus of Nazareth was none of these things, and accepting a crucified Messiah was just not in the cards. Saul fell along this line of thinking with the majority of the Jewish community. Saul did not know Jesus Christ, had never met him, and was not interested in his preaching or in following him.

As a young man of around 30 years of age, as he traveled on the road to Damascus, Saul had a vision. This vision was of the resurrected Jesus Christ, who had recently been crucified, and the vision revealed things to him. It also left him temporarily blind, taking three days to recover his sight. Following his revelation, Saul began referring to himself as Paul and preaching that Jesus was in fact the Jewish Messiah and the Son of God. He would spend the remainder of his life helping to establish the early Christian Church and seeking converts to Christianity.

Much of the doctrine and dogma of Christianity can be credited to Paul, although a lot of it is still debated today under the guise of theology (which means the study of made-up stuff). However, these are commonly accepted Christian doctrinal positions that were created by one man, following a "revelation."

- *Atonement:* The concept that followers of Christ are excused from the Mosaic Law handed to Moses by God, and can be cleansed of sin by Jesus' death. His death was a sacrifice and his blood made peace between God and mankind. The act of baptism allows one to share in Jesus' death and resurrection, and become cleansed of sin.

- *Salvation:* Paul wrote that faith in Christ was sufficient for salvation and that the Torah did not bind the followers of Jesus. He argued that those who chose Christianity did not need to first become Jewish, follow the dietary restrictions, rules or otherwise follow Mosaic Law.

Additionally, Paul's writings were credited with making Jesus divine, creating the concept of Original Sin, as well as the concept of transubstantiation (the magical turning of bread and wine into the literal body and blood of Christ), and shifting emphasis from an Earthly Kingdom of God to a Heavenly Kingdom. One of the central themes that Paul espoused was faith in Jesus as the most important requirement, which is certainly a concept that resonates loudly through Christianity today.

Around the year 50, early Church leaders met in Jerusalem and concurred with Paul that converts to Christianity would not need to be circumcised and become Jews first, and that the Laws of Moses would generally not apply to Christians. The Council of Jerusalem, as it is called, did agree to keep a few restrictions in place, namely fornication, idolatry, eating meat with blood in it and eating meat from animals not properly slain. Future Church leaders would expand on this theme of replacement of the Old Covenant with God by the New Covenant with God and emphasize again that faith in Christ is the necessary component for salvation and peace with God.

Christianity spread throughout the area into places like Syria, Mesopotamia, Jordan and Egypt but got its biggest boost when Emperor Constantine decided he liked it quite a bit and made it the official religion of the Roman Empire. During the Middle Ages it became common throughout Europe and continued to spread as Europeans began exploring the world. While the Crusades, Inquisitions, heresy hunts and witch burning would come later, spreading Christianity at the point of a sword, early Christianity seems to have spread because it promised a resurrection of the dead along with eternal life, at the low price of putting your faith in Jesus. No circumcision necessary.

As I stated in the Preface, I was indoctrinated into the Roman Catholic version of Christianity and while I left the church as a teenager, I never fully explored what I'd been taught. Instead, I tried to ignore it, poking fun at some of the more ludicrous concepts when they came up, but really not having the information necessary to finally break free from all of it and see it as the transparent nonsense that it is. While I've essentially made my peace with all the threats of eternal damnation, the instruction to beseech the Lord for mercy and my feelings of perpetual sinfulness, learning about Saul of Tarsus really raised my ire. I have to believe that someone in a position of authority, a priest or Monsignor, surely knew that one man made up the Christian ideology, 2,000 years ago, after having some kind of apoplectic episode. One guy, writing a few ideas on a piece of paper after a hallucination, during a time when we thought disease was caused by demonic possession. On this basis you've set up this entire system of churches, schools, hospitals, hierarchy and tithing? Shame on you.

I'd like to think that any rational person who does a bit of research into the origins of things they believe in will often have the following epiphany: we believe a lot of nonsense. Our history is littered with ideas that get passed along from generation to generation, by family, friends, neighbors, media, etc. Superstitions that we all know, that a black cat crossing your path is bad luck for example, started somewhere and struck a chord in the human psyche and have lasted for hundreds, if not thousands of years. Something as common as saying Bless You when a person sneezes has a superstitious origin that once learned, makes it difficult to say with a straight face.

Saul of Tarsus may have been convinced by his retinal migraine that he'd been visited by the Son of the Creator of the Universe, but anyone else who could be convinced of something that improbable based solely on one man's hallucinatory tale, and then allow those ideas to form a worldview, would, I'd argue, believe literally anything.

~~*~~

15. The Nicene Creed

A creed is a statement of belief. The Nicene Creed is one of the world's most famous and is a summary of the orthodox faith of the Christian Church and is used in the liturgy of most Christian Churches. The point of the creed is to unite all Christians in the core beliefs by capturing them in one document and having it read repeatedly, sometimes by the entire congregation. It was originally drawn up in the year 325 and revised in 381, so it's just about as old as the Christian faith. As a child, I spent years mindlessly reciting it, but by breaking it down for this book, I've applied some mental elbow grease to see what it's really about.

"We believe in one God, the Father, the Almighty maker of heaven and earth, of all that is seen and unseen."

That is a clear and concise opening statement that sticks with the Old Testament and the First Commandment.

"We believe in one Lord, Jesus Christ, the only Son of God, eternally begotten of the Father, God from God, Light from Light, true God from true God, begotten, not made, one in Being with the Father."

That's some odd language which begs the question, what? Well, the priests of the time were in serious debate about whether Jesus was the Son of God and therefore subordinate to him. The majority of priests wanted Jesus <u>to be</u> God. You can see how this would be a problem as the Lord was pretty clear that there should be no gods before Him. So, they agreed to say that Jesus was begotten by the Father (sired by him) but added the "*God from God*" language, and then emphasized it redundantly with "*true God from true God*" and threw in the final reminder that he was sired by God, not made by Him, and that He was one with Him. No confusion there.

"*Through him all things were made. For us men and for our salvation he came down from heaven by the power of the Holy Spirit he was born of the Virgin Mary, and became man.*"

Here, the early Christians were trying to solidify their message, namely that Jesus, while being born a man, was still God since all things were made through him. That his purpose for coming from heaven was to save mankind (from the Original Sin of Adam and Eve) and finally, that his mother was a virgin.

"*For our sake he was crucified under Pontius Pilate; he suffered, died, and was buried. On the third day he rose again in fulfillment of the Scriptures; he ascended into heaven and is seated at the right hand of the Father.*"

So here we are reminded that although the Son of God was killed, he rose from the dead. The fulfillment of the Scriptures part is interesting as it's his own words he's fulfilling. Jesus told his disciples that just like Jonah was in the whale for three days, he'd be in the ground for three days. The ascension is also added here, and the odd Father & Son seating arrangement is confirmed. I say it's odd because the Christians wanted so desperately to have Jesus be God, but they didn't want to be polytheists. In other words, they didn't want multiple gods to worship so they had to come up with a way for Jesus to be God, and somehow still be His Son. It would have been a lot easier if they had just said that Jesus was God in the flesh.

"He will come again in glory to judge the living and the dead, and his kingdom will have no end."

Here the Christians line up with their Jewish and Muslim brethren in predicting the rising of the dead. This is a central theme for all three of the Abrahamic religions; that at the end of our time on Earth, the dead will rise. They're non-specific on how this occurs or in what condition the dead will be when they rise. Are they literally corpses, skeletons and ashes? Are those who died as babies resurrected as babies? It's a truly gruesome aspect of these religions, and shows a fairly transparent preoccupation with our mortality.

"We believe in the Holy Spirit, the Lord, the giver of Life, who proceeds from the Father and the Son. With the Father and the Son he is worshiped and glorified. He has spoken through the Prophets. We believe in one holy catholic and apostolic Church. We acknowledge one baptism for the forgiveness of sins. We look for the resurrection of the dead, and the life of the world to come. Amen."

The wrap-up features the Holy Spirit again, not seen since he was sent from heaven to visit Mary, but for some reason the Christians really complicate things by elevating him to God. I guess I understand he is God's Spirit, but then why not just say that, rather than make the Holy Spirit another element of the already confusing Godhead? He's the giver of life, which presumably is impregnating Mary to bring Jesus to life, but they also say he proceeds from God and Jesus. Finally, they add him to the trio by saying that he is also to be worshipped and glorified. Not to be left out of the picture, the early Church includes itself in the Creed and says it's the one and only one Christians believe in, and then acknowledges that we're all looking toward End Times and the walking dead.

Four times in the Creed is the phrase "we believe." Nowhere in the Creed is there any rationale given for the belief. It just is. The Catholic Church has steadfastly held onto the Creed, but other Christian denominations don't think much of it and don't recite it.

So what are we to make of this Creed, this statement of belief that Christians the world over hold as the core message of their faith? I think it shows fairly clearly that Christianity was fumbling along 300 years after Christ's death until the power brokers of the time cobbled together this statement, which they argued over for over half a century, so they could coalesce around a repeatable message. It also shows a complete lack of evidentiary requirements as the Council of Nicaea basically chose the language they wanted to use to represent their belief system, ensuring that Jesus would be seen as God, not as a separate entity.

The Council also decided one more important element of Christianity; when Easter would be celebrated. The council decided to celebrate Easter on the first Sunday after the first full moon following the vernal equinox.

Ironically, the Council was called together by a Roman Emperor. Constantine the Great, trying to bring order to the various religious sects and beliefs in Rome asked bishops to gather together to come up with a unified position. Constantine also decreed that anyone could worship any deity they wanted without fear of persecution. It wasn't all halos and crucifixes though as a group of Christians in North Africa wouldn't conform and Constantine took an Army of Christian soldiers to war against the rebels. He believed in conformity and stability.

So now you know another bit of the history of Christianity. A Roman Emperor, trying to bring order to a fractious society, called Christian bishops to town and asked them to get their act together and unify the belief system. 325 years after Christ's death, the religion that bears his name solidified their position statement and Christians to this day still recite what they "believe" just like Constantine envisioned that they would.

~~*~~

16. The Resurrection Myth

There is nothing more certain in the life of a human being than death. Every human being who has lived during the 200,000 years of our existence on this planet has died or is dying. It is still joked that nothing is certain except for death and taxes, but I think the evidence will support that taxes can in fact be avoided. Not so with death. The incredible advancements in science and medicine have slowly pushed the average life expectancy in an upward trajectory, but science cannot prolong the human life indefinitely, nor has science ever brought a truly dead human back to life. For those who will argue the contrary, that we have in fact restored human beings to life after being "dead" for a short period, the answer is simple: they weren't dead.

Easter marks the day that Christians the world over commemorate the resurrection of Jesus Christ from the dead. As we just discussed, The Council of Nicaea selected the date in 325, during the time of the Roman Empire when the Nicene Creed was also written. After being dead for three days, Jesus appeared outside his tomb, in varying versions of the tale from the four Biblical Gospels, and spoke with his followers before ultimately flying off the face of the Earth into Heaven to be seated at the right hand of the Father.

Christopher Hitchens, of whom I am an unabashed fan, told various versions of what I am about to paraphrase during debates whenever the topic of Biblical miracles came up. In order to get the full impact of the argument that follows, it's important to remember that the Gospels were not written during Christ's lifetime. They were all written many decades after his death by unknown authors. There is no argument here as scholars have confirmed these facts repeatedly. There is no contemporary writing of the life and times of Jesus Christ anywhere in the world. The first mention of him is in Paul's letters to the Churches of Galatia, and scholars have dated them to approximately the year 49.

If you were to witness something yourself, which required the suspension of the laws of nature, for example seeing a man walking the streets whom you had seen executed just three days earlier, you would have to ask yourself the following question: What is more probable; that the laws of nature have been suspended in this one instance, or that you are under some misapprehension? Anyone in this situation would have to ask himself or herself this, and this is *if you had seen it with your own eyes*. If you are taking it instead on a report from others, who were also non-eyewitnesses, passed along through generations in ancient texts, then you are essentially advertising that you'll believe anything.

What should increase your skepticism of these accounts, apart from the rather obvious impossibility of a reanimated corpse, is that the resurrection of the dead seemed quite common at the time. Lazarus was raised from the dead and left to walk away without even an interview to capture what he had experienced. Jairus, a ruler of a synagogue, whose 12-year old daughter had died, saw his daughter also restored to life and not another word was spoken of it. Upon Jesus' death, there was a great earthquake, the temple veil was torn in two and tombs split open, with the reanimated corpses of many men going into the city to appear to many people. There was no reporting of this unusual event, no attempts to talk to the living dead and no information regarding what they did with their newly restored lives.

Human beings are storytellers; this much is obvious. For some it comes incredibly naturally, with even children whipping up fictitious tales with uncanny ease. Scattered throughout the history of mankind are tales of myth, legend and heroics, from the complete fabrication of William Tell, a national hero in Switzerland, to the false account of George Washington's cherry tree incident. Who has not heard tell of Robin Hood, who stole from the rich and gave to the poor? Yet the evidence that such a person ever existed is remarkably thin, relegating him to the pile of legendary folk heroes.

Could there have been a Jewish preacher in the remote region of Palestine who had a small following of fishermen and goat herders? Certainly, but just as there could have been an outlaw in the time of King John, who had a small band of merry men robbing the rich as they traveled through Sherwood Forest, the tales grew into legend and myth as they were told and retold.

A myth is a traditional story of seemingly genuine historical events that serves to unfold part of the worldview of a people or explain a practice or a belief system. With no evidence to support that a man named Jesus Christ every lived, nothing we can point to and confirm his existence, how credible is the idea that these stories of a man who cured lepers, restored sight to the blind, raised the dead to life again, and ultimately raised himself from the dead are true? Like Moses before him who parted the Red Sea and received tablets of stone from a tribal god named Yahweh, or Joshua, for whom the sun stood still in the sky so that he could complete his tribal battle in daylight, or Jonah who lived in the belly of a whale for three days, the story of the resurrected Jesus Christ falls high on the scale of improbability, and belongs more assuredly beside the stories of Apollo, the son of Zeus.

A challenge for believers

Dan Barker was a Christian preacher with a degree in Religion from Azusa Pacific University until he left Christianity in 1984. Mr. Barker is the co-President of the Freedom from Religion Foundation and on Easter Sunday, 2013, I was fortunate enough to come across his challenge to Christians to stand up for the core belief in Christianity: The Resurrection of Jesus Christ.

The challenge is to read the 6 sections of the Bible that describe the events from the resurrection to the ascension of Christ into heaven. It's only 165 verses in total, between the four Gospels and two sections written by Saul of Tarsus. You should take notes of the events described, and then in your own words, write a chronology of the events as the Bible describes them. If you've never done this before, I think you'll find it enlightening and a bit shocking. I provide a link to the Easter Challenge in the Appendix.

~~*~~

17. Was the Holy Trinity a plagiarism?

The Christian concept of the Holy Trinity was codified in the fourth century during the Council of Nicaea, but a man named Tertullian first invented it in the third century. He wrote that God the Father, God the Son and the Holy Spirit were one in essence, not in person. The Council tried to make that more clear, but as we've seen, the Nicene Creed's language is equally confusing, stating that Jesus Christ was begotten not made, being of one substance with the Father. How did all of this originate and perhaps more interestingly, why?

The Biblical God Yahweh or Jehovah is the one God of monotheism, and He made it clear that He was a jealous God and that man was to have no gods before Him. In the Torah, which are the first five books of the Bible, the prayers begin with *"Here, Oh Israel: The Lord is our God, the Lord is one."* However, when Jesus allegedly told his disciples to *"go therefore and make disciples of all nations, baptizing them in the name of the Father and of the Son and of the Holy Spirit,"* it certainly made it seem that there were three deities, not one.

Of the four Gospels, John is distinct in that it makes the case that Jesus is God, stating that through him all things were made, and even quotes Jesus as saying that he is one with the Father. While the Gospel of Matthew doesn't come close to John's declarations of Christ's divinity, it does quote Jesus as saying that all things had been handed over to him by his Father. Saul of Tarsus, of whom we've recently discussed authored much of Christian theology, included several statements that would seek to attribute divinity to Jesus, including giving him credit for the creation of all things in heaven and on earth, visible and invisible. Paul wrote the following blessing in Corinthians: *"The grace of the Lord Jesus Christ, and the love of God, and the communion of the Holy Ghost, be with you all. Amen."* This further added to the seeming trifecta of godliness that had to be reconciled with the one God concept.

Early Christian leaders argued over the nature of the Father, Son and Holy Spirit, creating many schisms and debating philosophies. The various creeds were formed as a means to bring Christian thinking together into a cohesive doctrine. The overarching view is that the three—Father, Son and Holy Spirit–share one essence or substance. God the Father is manifest in Jesus Christ, who offers the one salvation, to whom we have access because of the Holy Spirit. Some Christians go further to state that Jesus, in addition to being part of the three-headed God also has dual natures: fully God and fully human. The Athanasian Creed is more specific regarding the nature of the Trinity than either the Nicene Creed or the Apostles Creed and states in part:

*"That we worship one God in Trinity, and Trinity in Unity;
Neither confounding the Persons; nor dividing the Essence. For
there is one Person of the Father; another of the Son; and another of
the Holy Ghost. But the Godhead of the Father, of the Son, and of the
Holy Ghost, is all one; the Glory equal, the Majesty coeternal. Such
as the Father is; such is the Son; and such is the Holy Ghost. The
Father uncreated; the Son uncreated; and the Holy Ghost uncreated.
The Father unlimited; the Son unlimited; and the Holy Ghost
unlimited. The Father eternal; the Son eternal; and the Holy Ghost
eternal. And yet they are not three eternals; but one eternal."*

There are Christian denominations who don't believe in the
concept of the Trinity, with the Jehovah's Witnesses being the
most well known. The other religions that follow the Biblical
God, Judaism and Islam, have called the Trinity absurd,
incompatible with monotheism and owing more to pagan
religions than anything else. It is to this latter statement that I
wish to expand upon as seeking the origins of ideas and
concepts can help us in our quest for truth.

- Moirai, The Fates, were the Greek Gods of destiny:
  Clotho, Lachesis and Atropos.

- The Norns of Norse Mythology were three powerful
  giants, Uror, Veroandi and Skuld who weave the
  threads of destiny and are entwined with the flow
  of time.

- The Matres were a triad of goddesses who seem to have
  been worshipped in areas occupied by the Roman
  Empire's armies in the early 1st century.

- Diana Nemorensis was a triune goddess of the
  ancient peoples of Italy, hundreds of years before the
  time of Christ.

- In ancient Egypt, there were many triune gods
  including the sun god Ra, who had three different
  aspects or forms: Kheper in the morning, Re-
  Horakhty at noon and Atum in the evenings.

- And of course, Hinduism, which is much older than Christianity, features the holy trinity of Brahma, Vishnu and Shiva.

Could the Christian Trinity be a basic plagiarism? Tertullian, who first put forth the Trinitarian concept, was a son of a Roman centurion, was raised in Carthage and appears to have been trained in Roman law. He wrote books in Greek and was very familiar with Greek theology. He certainly would be familiar with the triune gods and goddesses of the pre-Christian era. Polytheism was the norm in many ancient cultures, but the early Christians were Jews, and therefore monotheists. Jesus was thought to be the Jewish Messiah by some, but this was met with scorn from Jewish leaders since Jesus did not meet the qualifications to be the Messiah. The early Christians did not wish to be polytheists, worshipping multiple gods, so there had to be a way to encompass the Old Testament God, Jesus Christ and the oft-mentioned Holy Spirit into the same God. A trinity of holiness was an indecipherable, but easy, solution.

It would appear that, just as with the virgin birth of Jesus, the idea of a triune Godhead was nothing new, but merely a repackaging of existing ideas from the early days of mankind's struggles to comprehend our world.

~~*~~

18. It's just a theory

If I accomplish nothing more with this book than to clarify once and for all for my readers what is meant by the term "theory" when it comes to scientific discussion, I will feel a deep sense of satisfaction. There is no excuse for making the statement, "it's just a theory" when the topic of evolution comes up. All it does is show that the person who utters it is willfully ignorant, and when I say willfully, that is precisely what I mean. In a few moments on the Internet, one can educate themselves as to what is meant by the use of the term "theory" relative to all things scientific.

When Charles Darwin first came up with his remarkable idea that the wide variation of plant and animal life on Earth could be a result of natural processes of selection for the variation most adaptable to its environment, it was not a theory. It was an idea, a guess if you will. When Girolamo Fracastoro proposed that diseases were caused by seed-like entities, it was an idea to counter the prevailing thought at the time, which was that disease was caused by bad air or poisonous vapors. It was not a theory.

Only when an explanation for some aspect of our natural world has been confirmed through repeated observation and experimentation can it be considered a theory. Theories continue to improve as more evidence is gathered and the power of a theory is in its ability to make predictions. In other words, if the theory of evolution through natural selection is correct, we predict that we will find fossils of now extinct species that may resemble current living species buried in the Earth's surface. And of course, we have found them and continue to find them. The story of how a transitional species from fish to land creature was discovered still give me chills to read and it's a perfect example of what I mean by the predictive power of scientific theory.

I first read of the discovery of Tiktaalik in Jerry Coyne's "Why Evolution is True," a book I highly recommend. As Jerry writes, *"one of the greatest fulfilled predictions of evolutionary biology is the discovery, in 2004, of a transitional form between fish and amphibians. This is the fossil species Tiktaalik roseae, which tells us a lot about how vertebrates came to live on the land. Its discovery is a stunning vindication of the theory of evolution. Until about 390 million years ago, the only vertebrates were fish. But, 30 million years later, we find creatures that are clearly tetrapods: four-footed vertebrates that walked on land. These early tetrapods were like modern amphibians in several ways: they had flat heads and bodies, a distinct neck, and well-developed legs and limb girdles. Yet they also show strong links with earlier fishes, particularly the group known as "lobe-finned fishes," so called because of their large bony fins that enabled them to prop themselves up on the bottom of shallow lakes or streams. The fishlike structures of early tetrapods include scales, limb bones, and head bones.*

How did early fish evolve to survive on land? This was the question that interested – or rather obsessed – my University of Chicago colleague Neil Shubin. Neil had spent years studying the evolution of limbs from fins, and was driven to understand the earliest stages of that evolution. This is where the prediction comes in. If there were lobe-finned fishes but no terrestrial vertebrates 390 million years ago, and clearly terrestrial vertebrates 360 million years ago, where would you expect to find the transitional forms? Somewhere in between. Following this logic, Shubin predicted that if transitional forms existed, their fossils would be found in strata around 375 million years old. Moreover, the rocks would have to be from freshwater rather than marine sediments, because late lobe-finned fish and early amphibians both lived in fresh water.

Searching his college geology textbook for a map of exposed freshwater sediments of the right age, Shubin and his colleagues zeroed in on a paleontologically unexplored region of the Canadian Arctic: Ellesmere Island, which sits in the Arctic Ocean north of Canada. And after five long years of fruitless and expensive searching, they finally hit pay dirt: a group of fossil skeletons stacked one atop another in sedimentary rock from an ancient stream. When Shubin first saw the fossil face poking out of the rock, he knew that he had at last found his transitional form. In honor of the local Inuit people and the donor who helped fund the expeditions, the fossil was named Tiktaalik roseae ("Tiktaalik" means "large freshwater fish" in Inuit, and "roseae" is a cryptic reference to the anonymous donor)."

- Coyne, Jerry A. (2009-01-22). Why Evolution Is True. Penguin Group. Kindle Edition.

Scientific theories are the most reliable form of scientific knowledge. Gravity is a theory, as is the theory that the Earth revolves around the Sun. In other words, scientific theories are facts about the natural world we live in. They have been proven to be predictive, accurate and perhaps most importantly, they have not been disproven. A central characteristic of science and scientific thinking is falsifiability. A scientific theory can be shown as flawed if it can be disproved by experiment or observation. Let us take evolution as an example, as in my next argument, I will show that evolution does a pretty compelling job of disproving Christianity (which is not a theory by the way). How could the theory of evolution be shown to be flawed or false?

The first thing we should look at is what evolutionary theory predicts. Evolution tells us that there will be variation in species and that the most adaptable of those variations will be selected naturally, and that traits can be passed along through heredity. If it could be shown that genetic mutations for example, do not occur, it would destroy the theory. If it could be shown that genetic mutations aren't passed along to offspring, it would destroy the theory. If it could be shown that environmental pressures do not favor the reproductive success of the better-suited variations of individual species, it would destroy the theory. As geneticist and evolutionary biologist John Haldane once quipped, finding fossilized rabbits in the Precambrian layer of the Earth would destroy his confidence in the theory of evolution. The reason this half-joking response to a question still resonates, is because rabbits are mammals, and evolutionary theory tells us that mammals emerged as a class of animal hundreds of millions of years after the Precambrian period of Earth's history. So if mammal fossils were found in the Precambrian layer of the Earth, suggesting that they lived hundreds of millions of years earlier than the theory of evolution predicts they would have, the theory would be in trouble.

The theory of evolution has never been disproven despite over 150 years of attempting to do just that. Instead over a century of experiments and observations have confirmed its truth and with it, the incredible and wonderful tale that is life on Earth. If you ever wish to sink your teeth into something worthwhile and take the time to learn and study a topic, I can find no more rewarding suggestion than the study of how life evolves. As promised, I'll now make the case that evolution does a nice job of showing that Christianity is not a logical and tenable candidate for truthfulness.

~~*~~

19. Does evolution disprove Christianity?

I can make many arguments describing what I think are the harmful effects of faith-based belief in the supernatural, but the primary argument that I remain truly passionate about is that it's false. The Church is a business selling an invisible product-everlasting life in an invisible sky kingdom-that is only available after death. Consider this simple business model:

1. Create a problem: Sin

2. Create a solution: Jesus

3. Offer a product: Salvation

There is no need for a return counter, as no one will ever come back from the dead to complain that the product was not delivered upon. A customer can literally never go to their pastor or priest and demand a refund of the time, money and emotional energy exerted to support the church's business, as they cannot return from the dead to complain that the sky kingdom doesn't exist.

In order to make the argument that evolution actually disproves Christianity, let's look first at what Christian theology says about sin and the role Jesus plays in the salvation of mankind. The Catholic Church doctrine states that humans are born into a state of sin, distinct from sins they commit. They believe that baptism washes away that sin, which comes from Adam, the first man, who lost the original holiness and justice he had received from God, not only for himself but also for all humans. Adam and Eve transmitted human nature to their descendants, who were then wounded by that first sin and hence deprived of original holiness and justice; this deprivation is called "original sin."

John Calvin, who broke from the Catholic Church and became a Protestant Reformer believed humans inherited Adam's guilt and are in a state of total depravity from the moment of their birth. Redemption by Jesus Christ is the only remedy.

Methodists believe that Original Sin is the "corruption of the nature of every man, that naturally is engendered of the offspring of Adam, whereby man is very far gone from original righteousness, and of his own nature inclined to evil…"

Lutherans also believe in the fall of Adam, as do the Anglicans. The Mormons have a slightly different twist to their concept of The Fall, but still place the blame specifically on Adam, the first human.

What we know, thanks to the genius of Darwin and the work done by scientists in his wake over the last 150 years, is that new species of life only emerge extremely gradually. There is no first creature of any species. A platypus didn't instantly appear, becoming the first platypus. There was no animal that you could point to and say, "look, it's the first dog ever." The transition from one species to another is almost imperceptible, and that includes the transition from Homo heidelbergensis to Homo sapiens. In other words, there was no first man and first woman (Adam and Eve) in a perfect garden from which the entire population of Homo sapiens descended. Humans did not originate in the Garden of Eden but in Africa, and they were descendants of other hominins before them. We now know that some early humans left Africa and encountered Neanderthals in Europe and interbred with them. Human DNA has Neanderthal DNA in it, except for those humans whose ancestors remained in Africa.

Geneticists who study human evolution and population genetics theorize that the total population of Homo sapiens declined precipitously several times, to as low as perhaps 2,000 of us at one point, before we rebounded. But two Homo sapiens could not produce the amount of variation present in modern human genes. I'll also point out that if Eve was formed out of the rib of Adam, as Genesis tells us, then Eve was Adam's genetic clone. You can see how problematic that would be. I assume you can start to see the issue at hand. The true story of life on Earth as told by the theory of evolution and confirmed in the fossil record and the DNA record tells us that there was no "first man" and "first woman."

Since we know then that the Adam and Eve story is not true, there can be no Fall of Man from God's grace in the Garden of Eden, which is when God chose to punish Adam and Eve and their progeny. Without this "sinfulness" that God placed upon the descendants of Adam and Eve (one wonders why God would punish innocent lives who had nothing to do with the first couple's transgressions), there was no need for Jesus to be brutally tortured and murdered in a filthy human sacrifice to sooth God's thirst for vengeance. If that's the case, then the *entire basis* for Christianity--accepting Jesus as Lord and Savior to wash us of Original Sin and gain access to heaven--is wiped clean. There is no Original Sin because there was no Adam and Eve and no first couple and no Fall of Man. It is nothing more than a story. A story capitalized on by men who rose to power by preaching fear and selling false promises of eternity in the clouds, and then building on their business model by forced conversions, torture, imprisonment and death.

The Catholic Church has affirmed to its followers that parts of the Bible are not true. This is a rather startling admission from one of the oldest Christian Churches in the world. The hammer blows of science have forced those who once burned heretics at the stake to become heretics themselves. They specifically state that the first 11 Chapters of Genesis cannot be historical but at most may contain historical traces. What they fail to admit is that by taking that position, that in fact Genesis 3--The Temptation and Fall of Man — is not true, they have removed the entire basis for Original Sin, for the Sacrament of Baptism and for the redeeming death of Jesus Christ.

This helps to explain the earnest and vehement attacks against Evolution by the Evangelical Christians in the United States who believe in a conservative interpretation of the Bible, including the Fall of Man, Original Sin, and the substitutionary sacrifice of Jesus Christ to redeem mankind from that Original Sin. They are unwilling to look at the evidence for evolution for they know it destroys their beliefs, and as we discussed previously, deep-seated beliefs are incredibly hard to give up. Without Adam and Eve and the "sin" in the Garden of Eden, there would be no Fall of Man, no "total depravity" for humans to be born into and as a result, no need for God to send His Son to Earth to die for our sins and wipe the slate clean. In effect, the entire basis for Christianity evaporates into a fairy tale under the insurmountable weight of the evidence.

So does the theory of evolution prove that Christianity is false? I certainly think so, but you'll have to decide for yourself if the arguments and evidence I've just presented are compelling enough to make that conclusion.

~~ *~~

20. Put theology to the test

The rate of acquired knowledge attained by the human species since our appearance on Earth is a remarkable testament to our powers of cognition. Through painstaking research and testing we discovered that microscopic germs were infecting us and killing our species by the millions. We developed ways to stop the onslaught. Incessantly curious about the world around us, we set upon a course of discovery that has not only saved the lives of millions who would otherwise have perished, but has improved the quality of those lives. The hero of this story is science.

The men and women who dedicate their lives to scientific discovery have brought us wonders we take for granted today. Their discoveries spawn inventions they never considered as they sought to solve life's mysteries and the seemingly unanswerable questions before us. Observing their work with something less than appreciation has been an armada of religious clerics, sometimes disguising themselves as theologians.

The domain of the church on Earth has peaked and is now on the decline. There isn't a single religious denomination that can claim growth among its ranks in several decades. The largest growing demographic is now the non-religious, the agnostic and the atheist. Those who would attempt to maintain control of the minds of the populace see Science as the enemy. The clerics and their theological brethren have been engaged in this battle since the earliest days of man's enlightenment.

As far as mankind has come in our knowledge–and the growth rate is picking up speed–there are many things we still don't know. After all, there are almost countless areas of discovery where a curious mind can spend a lifetime in learning. This opens the door for the clerical attack on science as they attempt to insert God into the gaps in our knowledge.

Once a lay person understands the rigors of scientific methodology, the clerical arguments ring hollow as they present no alternative that could stand up to the same rigorous testing and falsification. But to the person who lacks scientific background, the theologian can spin a web of doubt that will trap the innocent would be student of knowledge in its sticky tendrils. There are various forms of attack the theologians will take, and some seem so demure as to be respectable. They may ask only that science and religion live harmoniously side-by-side, in concurrence. They may even acknowledge the magnificent advances man has made–praise the Lord–and insert God as the mechanism for each and every wonder that we've discovered about the natural world. Do not be fooled.

The clerical attack on the gaps in knowledge, while occasionally successful in maintaining the indoctrinated believer in their supernatural belief system, have no evidence to support them. They will not present evidence; that is not in their modus operandi. They will instead attempt to shoot holes in the science and the methodology, knowing full well that their positions could not stand up to the same methods they seek to undermine.

Take any religious answer to questions of life, the universe and everything, and attempt to test it for validity. The cleric will tell you that God created the Universe in six days. That is their hypothesis for the origin of the Universe. To test this, we would make observations of the natural world and see if their hypothesis accurately "predicted" these observations. If they do not, the hypothesis is shown to be false and discarded or reconstructed to try again. Some of the craftier theologians, knowing full well that this hypothesis is false, will use literary metaphor to say that "six days" was not meant to be literal, but rather metaphorical and could be many billions of years. But that is only one aspect of where the hypothesis fails. Where is the observed evidence of God's existence? Just look around you, the cleric "humbly" lies.

Clerics despise the theory of evolution more than any other scientific explanation, as it explains the diversity of life as it exists on our planet. Charles Darwin, in discovering that natural selection was the explanation for the diversity in species effectively destroyed the clerics wishful thinking that God had created all of life in its present form through the sheer power of His imagination. Darwin was just the beginning as man has very recently discovered the genome and the dawn of genetics has shattered all doubts of the shared origins of every species of life on Earth.

Scientists spend countless hours attempting to falsify existing theories. While this seems counterintuitive to the layperson, it is the nature of scientific discovery. More attempts have been made to falsify the theory of evolution over the last 150 years than perhaps any other scientific theory, yet these efforts have only shown even more evidence of its fundamental truth. Here, the theologians have focused their efforts and attack with rabid abandon. They write books whose only goal is to attack the science contained in books on evolutionary theory. Do they present their own theories for an alternative answer to the diversity of species on Earth? They present the same answer given by man since the dawn of our time on Earth: "God did it." There is nothing new in the cleric's argument, nothing substantive. They merely attempt to mock the science, mock the scientist and point to the collection of ancient parchments written during the time when germs ravaged the human species and elaborate rituals and sacrifices were made to appease the gods who had obviously become angry with man. "Here, here in these books that were selected and voted on by clerics thousands of years ago, here are the answers you seek!"

Rational and thinking humans, who today enjoy all the benefits of scientific advancement should ask only that the clerics support their positions with evidence and scientific rigor. The same evidence and scientific rigor the clerics demand of scientists would be a wonderful place to begin. The next time a cleric says that science has not yet discovered how the first life on earth began, ask them to test their theory of how God did it. In fact, just ask them to prove God's existence, using the same standards they demand of scientists.

Religion is dying, of that there is little doubt. Man is evolving beyond it and it will never again regain the position of power that it held for thousands of years, attaining wealth and land, building mammoth churches and launching Crusades to convert or destroy the non-believer. Personal belief in the supernatural is part of the human psyche and only through the basic concept of testing and looking for evidence can each individual shed these tendencies. The cleric who stands only to lose power and influence will fight to keep their foothold on our minds, not with their own testing and evidence of a contrary position, but with ignorance, mockery and playing to our fears of death and of the unknown. They will promise much—answered prayers and an immortal soul for starters—but they do not even attempt to test these ridiculous tenets in the hope that no one will ask them to. They will feign offense if one questions them and use thinly veiled threats of punishment from the Almighty for our insolence.

The theologian and their clerical foot soldiers should be embarrassed to step into the scientific realm and attempt to undermine the advancement of knowledge. Allowing them in and considering them alongside science is inviting the cobra into your home and hoping it won't strike. The theologian stands outside of science, peering in to the laboratory like a Peeping Tom, searching for a way in. If the theologian wants to stand side-by-side with science, they must begin to treat their beliefs as scientific hypotheses and begin testing them with the same resolute determination to falsify them that scientists do. We must stop the theologian and the cleric from attacking the science, and ask them instead to prove their own positions. Only by our own relentless counterassault on their attacks will we put an end to this foolishness designed only to confuse and delude us, for the sole purpose of keeping the clerics in power.

~~ *~~

21. The Power of Prayer

On March 5, 2011, the news media confirmed that a couple was sentenced to manslaughter for allowing their toddler to die from illness while they refused medical help, and prayed instead. This isn't the first such case, and I'm confident it won't be the last. There are Christians who believe wholeheartedly in the power of prayer and some to an extreme degree.

In the Bible, Jesus spoke of prayer often, and how anything was possible with God. He was very specific on many occasions:

- Matthew 21: *"Truly I tell you, if you have faith and do not doubt, you can say to this mountain, ' Go throw yourself into the sea' and it will be done. If you believe you will receive whatever you ask for in prayer."*

- Luke 11: *"So I say to you: Ask and it will be given to you; seek and you will find; knock and the door will be opened to you. For everyone who asks, receives; the one who seeks finds; and to the one who knocks, the door will be opened."*

- Mark 11:24 *"Therefore I tell you, whatever you ask for in prayer, believe that you have received it, and it will be yours."*

- John 14: *"And I will do whatever you ask in my name, so that the Father may be glorified in the Son. You may ask for anything in my name, and I will do it."*

- Matthew 18:19 *"Again, truly I tell you that if two of you on earth agree about anything they ask for, it will be done for them by my Father in heaven."*

And lastly, for those that argue that if your prayer was not answered, it's because your faith was not strong enough, let's see what Jesus had to say in that regard:

- Matthew 17:20 *"Truly I will tell you, if you have faith as small as a mustard seed, you can say to this mountain, 'Move from here to there,' and it will move. Nothing will be impossible for you."*

So I think I've established pretty clearly and with little room for debate that Christians believe in the power of prayer because Jesus himself, the Son of God, told them that through prayer, literally anything was possible.

People pray for all kinds of things. They ask for prayers for their friend, who is ill with cancer. They pray that their job interview will go well. They pray for the safety of their families. If we were to consider the effectiveness of prayer, all we'd really have to do is have a group of Christians pray for something specific and see what happens. As it turns out, that experiment has already been done.

A study was done with over 1,800 patients at six different hospitals around the United States. The patients had all received coronary bypass surgery. Researchers broke the patients into three groups: two were prayed for, one was not. Half of the group being prayed for was told they'd be prayed for, the others were not.

Three congregations–St Paul's Monastery, the Community of Teresian Carmelites in MA, and Silent Unity, a Missouri prayer ministry near Kansas City–were asked to pray for the patients and were given their first names and the initials of their last names. They were told they could pray however they wanted to, but asked them to include prayers "for a successful surgery with a quick, healthy recovery and no complications."

98

Researchers analyzed the patients' recovery after 30 days and the results were clear: prayer had no effect whatsoever. In fact, a higher number of patients who knew they were being prayed for suffered from complications. More patients in the group who received prayer but didn't know it had major complications.

Dr. Benson who had previously emphasized the soothing power of personal prayer led the study. The John Templeton Foundation that supports research into spirituality funded it.

At an annual meeting of Christian pastors the topic of prayer came up. A group of pastors were very discouraged that none of their prayers were being answered. One pastor confessed that in his 20 years of ministry, there was not one specific prayer he could point to that had ever been answered. Multiple pastors expressed their despair and frustration with prayer. The pastors leading the conference then proceeded to try to determine why these prayers went unanswered. One pastor, Francis Chan, suggested that those whose prayers hadn't been answered should check their marriages, their motives and their heart. Theologian John Piper went further and challenged pastors to examine all aspects of their lives. Piper: "*The Bible is clear: God is absolutely sovereign. … The Bible is just as clear that you have not because you asked not. Had you asked the universe would've been different,*" he explained. "*God knows you're going to pray or not; … if they happen, they were in the plan designed to unleash a hundred magnificent things. If they don't happen, those things don't get unleashed. This is not philosophically hard.*"

Jerry Rankin, president emeritus of the International Mission Board of the Southern Baptist Convention, pointed to the enemy–Satan–as one reason for the lack of effectiveness of prayer among many leaders. And the enemy works in subtle ways by causing busyness, discouragement, diversion, or distraction.

If we go back to what Jesus very specifically told us about prayer, we clearly see the dilemma. Prayer by three different Christian churches for what was clearly a noble cause had no effect. Pastors who dedicate their lives to Jesus and the Christian faith get no response to their prayers. Why did these prayers not work?

We should try to answer this question by choosing the answer that is the most direct, the simplest and the one that raises the fewest additional questions. Intercessory prayer has been clearly demonstrated to be ineffective. We can try to answer that question as the pastors and theologians did, by questioning the faith of those praying, their motives, suggesting that perhaps God had other plans, etc. Or we can answer by saying intercessory prayer is ineffective because no one is actually listening or interested in our prayers.

Which of those two possible answers is the simplest, most direct, most probable answer? Which of those two answers requires the fewest assumptions or raises the fewest additional questions? If you were honest with yourself, you'd have to answer the latter. Prayer doesn't work because we're praying to no one. There is no evidence of any kind to support that a deity is hearing our prayers and responding to them, answering them and interceding in human lives, despite what Jesus allegedly said (I say allegedly because all of the Gospels were written decades after the life of Jesus and we have no way of knowing if he ever said any of the things written in these Gospels). But if he did say them, he was either lying or delusional, since we have seen repeatedly that the prayers he told us would move mountains do nothing at all.

I'm not saying there is no personal benefit in prayer. But there's a difference between receiving personal solace and inner peace from praying, and praying for God to intervene in your life or the lives of others. If you still doubt me, and believe in what Jesus said about prayer in the Bible, then conduct your own experiment. Gather together with your fellow believers and pray for something very specific to occur and then see what happens.

~~*~~

22. Jesus and the Giant Game of Telephone

In the Middle East during the time of Jesus, much of the populace was illiterate. Education was reserved for the high of birth and stature. There is not a single word written by Jesus himself anywhere in the world. Not one. So it is safe to presume, since Jesus was not born into a royal family or one of great wealth, that he was most likely illiterate himself. Joseph was a carpenter by trade and Jesus aided him in his work. So where did the written record of his teachings come from?

The four Gospels of the New Testament tell us what we know about Jesus. All four of the Gospels were written in Greek and all were written at roughly the same time, i.e. 65 to 100 years after Jesus' birth. So the only records of Jesus and his teachings were written some 35 to 65 years after he died. The first mention of Jesus is in Paul's letters to the churches of Galatia, which scholars have dated to approximately the year 49. Paul never knew Jesus, writing based solely on revelation from Jesus' dead spirit. Were any of these documents written by people who actually knew Jesus, who were there to see the events they describe?

The Gospel of Matthew tells us of his lineage, his birth, his ministry and his ultimate death by crucifixion. Scholars still debate the actual author of this Gospel and most conclude the true author is unknown since there is no direct evidence of authorship. The original manuscripts have no author's name. So it would appear that the Gospel of Matthew, authored by an unknown individual or individuals, many decades after Jesus' death, was not written by an eyewitness to any of the events described. In fact, none of the writings even sound as if they were written by an eyewitness. Where did the information come from then?

Papias, an early leader of the Christian Church who was eventually canonized as a Saint, wrote about Jesus as well and he explained how he got his information. It was brought to him by travelers, who had heard it from others, who also had heard the stories from others, and so on, presumably eventually going back to someone who was an actual eyewitness of the events they describe.

So the Gospels, all four of them, were written in the same manner. In Greek, by relatively educated men, decades after the life and death of Jesus, based on accounts they heard told by others, who also heard the accounts told by others and so on. The Gospels themselves tell us there were only a dozen or so people who remained faithful to Jesus after his death and from these people the stories spread. Could these few people have traveled the world telling the tales of Jesus to everyone they could find to convert their listeners to Christianity? We know that Paul (formerly Saul) worked hard to establish new churches dedicated to Jesus, and asked others to spread the word. The stories were spread by word of mouth from town to town, city to city and country to country. Jesus, the miracle-working Son of God who died on the cross to bring salvation to all mankind was surely a powerful tale to tell in the first Century, but for hundreds of years Christianity faltered until Emperor Constantine adopted it as the religion of the Roman Empire.

Did you ever play telephone as a kid? You whisper a short, simple story in the ear of the person sitting next to you and they whisper it to the next person and so on until you get to the end and then compare stories. I tried a simple experiment a few moments ago and whispered to my daughter's boyfriend that a "giant red fish had leaped from the lake and swallowed a green grasshopper whole." We then chatted for a moment and I asked him to whisper it to my son. I then chatted them both up for a moment and asked my son to repeat what he'd been told. "A red fish jumped out of a green lake." Imagine if you will, people telling stories of Jesus as they traveled, as they encountered friends, as they broke bread and drank wine. Not over the course of a few minutes, but over 35 years. Then imagine an author, relatively educated, with leisure time to write. He has heard these stories told and finds them fascinating. He begins to write them down. Now imagine if you will, what resemblance his written word might have to actual events in another land, 35 years ago, of which there is no written record.

That is one giant game of telephone.

~~*~~

One frequently hears that the teachings of the alleged Jesus of Nazareth, Son of the Israeli Tribal God Yahweh, are to be held in high esteem. Certainly if he was the true Son of the Creator of the Universe, we'd be wise to follow his every teaching to the letter. But even those who don't support that supernatural claim at least believe his moral guidance serves as a compass for human actions. Mahatma Gandhi for example, wrote about Jesus that "...*he was certainly the highest example of one who wished to give everything, asking nothing in return, and not caring what creed might happen to be professed by the recipient.*" He went on to state that he believed Jesus to be one of the greatest teachers that humanity has ever had. Thomas Jefferson famously took a razor blade to the Bible and cut out all of the claims for the divinity of Jesus, the alleged miracles he performed, and anything that he felt could have been embellished by priests and those wishing to profit from Jesus. After doing so, Jefferson said "*there will be found remaining the most sublime and benevolent code of morals which has ever been offered to man.*"

In the Sermon on the Mount, which takes place early in the Ministry of Jesus, are contained the majority of his core teachings and are held by believers in Jesus as containing the core tenets of Christian discipleship. Augustine, an early church leader, had this to say about the Sermon:

"*If any one will piously and soberly consider the sermon which our Lord Jesus Christ spoke on the mount, as we read it in the Gospel according to Matthew, I think that he will find in it, so far as regards the highest morals, a perfect standard of the Christian life.*"

What I propose to do here is argue that the teachings of Jesus are not particularly noble, moral or useful, and that in fact putting much of it into practice is impossible. It's also important to me to state at the outset that we do not know if a man called Yeshua Ha'Netzeret (Jesus of Nazareth as he would have been known in Aramaic), claiming to be the Son of God, really said any of the things attributed to him. Jesus never put pen to paper himself, left behind nothing that we can point to as definitive of his life and his Ministry. The Gospels are where we find his words and they were authored by unknown men, decades after the death of Jesus and have been copied many times by hand. The original manuscripts are not in existence. The Gospels themselves have many discrepancies and contradictions casting further doubt upon the accounts contained therein. However, if we are to evaluate these so-called moral teachings, let alone the actual words of the Son of God, it is what we have to work with.

In the Beatitudes, Jesus made various proclamations regarding members of society seen as being among the less fortunate, and proclaimed them blessed. This does not strike me as a particularly creative or ingenious position--to look upon someone who is in mourning for example and take sympathy upon him or her.

- *"Blessed are those who mourn, for they will be comforted."*

The only thing we can take from this proclamation by Jesus is that when we see someone in mourning we should offer comfort. I'd venture a guess that prior to Jesus ever climbing up onto the mount and stating this, people had comforted each other in times of mourning. The other thing that strikes me as rather lame about these beatitudes is that there is no call to action, no activism or answer to the problem of suffering. All Jesus proclaims is that these poor souls are blessed, and then offers up some postmortem rewards and the outrageous promise to the meek that they will somehow inherit the earth, for which they remain in waiting.

Jesus then ensures the crowd who has gathered that the road to heaven is a challenging one, indicating that unless their righteousness surpasses that of the Pharisees and the teachers of the law, they will surely not enter heaven. This kind of stuff really gets my goat, as it's a common carrot and stick policy. It's designed to induce certain behavior in order to receive a reward, but there's a punishment on the other end which Jesus elaborates on later, that of eternal fire. How any self-respecting person can look at this as a noble teaching is difficult to understand. Jesus is making promises of life in an invisible celestial kingdom after death--a farfetched and dubious claim I'd say--if one's behavior were especially righteous. He doesn't show the stick here, only the carrot, but don't worry, the stick is coming.

Jesus confirms the preexisting admonition not to murder each other (I'm sure up until that moment, people felt that murder was A-Okay) and then adds this rather innocuous offense and brings out the aforementioned stick:

"But I tell you that anyone who is angry with a brother or sister will be subject to judgment. Again, anyone who says to a brother or sister, 'Raca,' is answerable to the court. And anyone who says, 'You fool!' will be in danger of the fire of hell."

I'll go out on a limb here and argue that while calling a brother or sister an empty-headed fool may be unpleasant in a childish kind of way, to threaten us with being roasted in flames for a bit of schoolyard anger with a friend cannot be held out as a compassionate and honorable position. Jesus really gets on a roll with the threats of everlasting heat stroke and third degree burns when he tells us that to even look at a woman with lust on your mind--which is a natural urge in all male human beings in order to ensure procreation and survival of the species--has already doomed you to being roasted like a marshmallow at a campfire. He goes so far as to offer this nugget of honorable, noble and compassionate wisdom:

"If your right eye causes you to stumble, gouge it out and throw it away. It is better for you to lose one part of your body than for your whole body to be thrown into hell. And if your right hand causes you to stumble, cut it off and throw it away. It is better for you to lose one part of your body than for your whole body to go into hell."

Let's keep in mind that Jesus alleges his Father, the Hebrew God, sent him and yet the Hebrew God never mentioned hell or eternal punishment. Sure, He'd have His preferred people slaughter everyone in a rival village, instruct them to take their virgin girls, their property and their land, but at least He left the dead alone. You never see Yahweh then torture the souls of the murdered indefinitely. No, the Prince of Peace brings the concept of damnation for eternity to the masses and somehow people hold this up as moral.

The "turn the other cheek" bit is really infuriating to me for this reason: not only is it a suggestion that is almost impossible to follow, it is one that we shouldn't follow. If we were to follow Jesus' guidance here, the bullies and thugs would prosper and thrive. It would become quite advantageous in fact to take up the practice as Jesus asks us to surrender to those who would do us harm, and also to do so willingly and even to give more than what they would take from us. I'd argue that those who claim the United States as a Christian Nation would have to admit that the US flagrantly disregards their leader's guidance as a matter of foreign policy.

Let's talk a bit about the charitable concepts that Jesus brings forth next in the Sermon. Churches around the world conduct charitable efforts in the name of Jesus--and take the opportunity to do some proselytizing as well--and charity is generally perceived as something positive. I don't know that Jesus invented the concept of charity, but his suggestion to give privately, in secret, is very troubling. Not only is it frequently disregarded, which is surprising since the Son of God instructed his followers to do so, but it fails to capitalize on one of the most effective means of leadership: leading by example. I'd argue that our charitable works should be public and the reason they are is because they're more effective in that way and we figured that out for ourselves, even though Jesus taught us otherwise.

One of the teachings of Jesus that I really like is sadly also ignored by his followers and I fervently wish they'd get with the program and follow their leader's guidance. Jesus tells us to pray silently, in our rooms with the door closed, not out in the streets and in the churches (although being a Jew, he used synagogues in his Sermon. Six of one, half-dozen of the other). He also tells us not to babble on like fools in our prayers to God, but to keep it short and simple. If Jesus is the Son of God and the only way to heaven is through him, then why on earth are his followers disobeying him so flagrantly? Even if he is seen only as a moral teacher, and his guidance held out as exemplary, why aren't those who choose to follow him actually following his guidance? Please Christians, listen to Jesus and stop your public displays of beseeching. It's not what he wanted.

Jesus admonishes those who would gather up riches that they cannot serve both God and money, and that people shouldn't worry about food, clothing and shelter. I'm not sure that this is particularly sound advice from the man, and it certainly isn't displayed by the masses. We spend the large majority of our time worrying about food, clothing and shelter so that we don't suffer miserably and die! Come on Jesus.

Jesus asks us to judge not, lest we be judged, which on the face of it sounds pretty noble and righteous and so forth. However, in practical terms, we must make judgments about others all the time. The wisest of us will make those judgments after gathering the needed information so that we can be confident of our position, whether it is to hire the person to our employ, take them on as a friend and confidant, or perhaps to pursue a business relationship with them. Certainly we should make careful judgments about those we entrust with our love or be prepared to pay a steep price for our folly.

Jesus then spends an inordinate amount of time preaching to us about how we can enter the invisible celestial kingdom for the dead. He claims that by asking, we will receive because God will provide. He again tells us how hard it is to get into the magic kingdom, since we have to find the small gate and the narrow road and that few of us will find it. He warns us of false prophets, again letting us know we're likely to be fooled and taken advantage of in this life, and that if we don't follow the will of God, Jesus will pretend not to know us when we come before God to enter the sky kingdom. He ends with yet another threat; that those who fail to follow his words are in deep trouble:

"But everyone who hears these words of mine and does not put them into practice is like a foolish man who built his house on sand. The rain came down, the streams rose, and the winds blew and beat against that house, and it fell with a great crash."

Let us set aside for a moment whether or not Jesus of Nazareth was born of a virgin who was inseminated by God's Holy Spirit, and whether he was ultimately murdered in a filthy, bloody human sacrifice to appease his Father after he'd spent some time walking around Bronze Age Palestine giving out the advice I've listed here. Let's just take up the teachings and evaluate them to determine where they stand in terms of the wise counsel humans have offered each other since the advent of language. If we remove the promises of an afterlife, for which there is no evidence even today, let alone 2,000 years ago when Jesus was preaching, and look only at what is left, my argument is that it is surprisingly little.

- The Beatitudes are nothing more than words of sympathy for the less fortunate.

- Calling on us not to murder each other is fairly obvious.

- Sure, adultery is bad, but we're only human.

- Surrendering to bullies, thieves, thugs and those who would take advantage of us is just bad advice.

- Love your enemies? Not only is this is a truly challenging proposition, but a dangerous one. They're your enemies for a reason.

- Being charitable privately is not particularly effective. At best, it's a pitch to be humble in your giving, and that's admirable, but on the whole, we're better off being openly charitable to show others the way.

- Throwing caution to the wind and not preparing for the future or worrying about feeding and clothing yourself is utter foolishness.

- If Jesus had taught us not to be quick to judge, but instead to be thoughtful and diligent in our judgments, I'd give him some props. But he didn't.

I have laid out my arguments for your consideration in regards to the teachings of Jesus. I don't think they add up to much and honestly, the promised rewards and threats of punishment after we die are really off-putting. Contrast this with say the counsel of Socrates. Socrates gave us a philosophy of ethics as a way to discover how we should live if we were to be truly fulfilled and successful human beings. He believed that the unexamined life was not worth living and thought it extremely important to know who we were and what we were trying to become. He deemed this necessary to lead a responsible and fully awake life for if you did not try to figure out who you were and what you believed then it would be as if you were content to just exist and what would be the point in that? Where would the value be in your existence? Socrates taught us to care for our essence, which he said was the basis for our thoughts, feelings, values, and decisions. His proposed way of keeping that essence healthy was by introspection and ridding oneself of ignorance. I'd argue that this sage of philosophy gave us something to really dig our teeth into with just those small nuggets of wisdom, and he didn't use a carrot or a stick to do it.

~~*~~

24. Where was God?

As the horror in Connecticut unfolded in mid-December of 2012, I knew it wouldn't be long before we'd hear people speak of God. The former Governor of Arkansas and then FOX News pundit Mike Huckabee was quick to blame the lack of God in schools as the reason that a madman, armed to the teeth, forced his way into an elementary school and murdered innocent children. As expected, the parents whose children did not take a lunatic's bullet were quick to claim it a miracle that their child survived the tragic, senseless violence. Our politicians, honestly the only ones who can take real action to change the ease with which any American can build themselves an arsenal of deadly weapons, decided to pray. What exactly they were praying for is anyone's guess. What prayers could be offered to a Supreme Being after a mass murder of this caliber? Were they prayers for the dead, or for the living?

The world's history is replete with unspeakable tragedy that God's most beloved creations have endured. All of the beseeching, begging and pleading for mercy, for intervention, has gone unanswered. The Lord God in Heaven has never stopped genocide, has never cared to prevent the starvation of children, has never intervened in a war, a death camp, a torture or a calamitous natural disaster. No, the omniscient and omnipotent Father in the sky knows every horror that will occur, every wail of terror, every child's desperate last moments and watches with indifference. He has watched as we were maimed and killed of polio, as the Black Death spread across Europe killing millions from flea-bitten rats spreading death, while the clerics prayed and prayed. Small pox agonized children until scientists saved them. Think of how many prayers, how much begging the Lord God Almighty must have heard from His chosen people as the Nazis exterminated them. Not a powerful finger did He lift to provide aid. In the long, tragic history of human suffering, a few murdered teachers and children could not possibly shock the senses of the All Powerful and All Loving God.

Some will claim that this is all part of a Divine Plan, one mere mortals cannot understand. They will claim that these children live on in the spirit world, their invisible and undetectable souls are now with God in Heaven. Some will even utter the cowardly and disgraceful words that the murdered are in a better place now. These platitudes are nothing more than excuses we make for our Heavenly Father's failure to take action. His abject and miserable failure.

The cold, hard reality is that we are all born into a losing struggle. No one here gets out alive. Through valiant efforts we have clawed our way out of our humble beginnings, when we were often food for wild beasts in the plains and jungles of Africa, to create medical marvels to stop the ravaging diseases our Creator let loose upon us. In a rich and prosperous land like the United States, even a citizen of average means lives like a proverbial king compared to much of the poverty stricken world. But the Lord displays the same aloof and distant approach with the US as He does with the Holy Land of Israel where the parties of God kill each other's children over the same promised patch of dirt.

Our Father in Heaven is either preposterously inept, callously indifferent, or completely imaginary. Accepting that He is imaginary is much less insulting than either of the other options. Where was God when a madman rained death upon innocent children in CT? The same place He's always been in times of madness, chaos and despair: In our imaginations.

~~*~~

The end of arguments

I have stated my case using what I think to be reasoned and logical arguments that demonstrate that human beings are the creators of gods and spirit worlds. You will be the ultimate judge as to whether my case is convincing or has at least provided some fertilizer for thinking about the issue. In Part II of the book, I will move from argument to evidence to attempt to prove beyond a reasonable doubt that God is a figment of our imaginations. He lives only in myths and legends authored by men in the Iron Age and perpetuated by men in the ensuing centuries.

Can an All-Powerful being create a Black Hole whose gravitational pull is so fierce, that even He cannot escape it? If He cannot create it, He is not All-Powerful. If He can create it and cannot escape it, then He is not All-Powerful. Therefore, an All-Powerful being cannot exist.

~~*~~

Part II - Evidence

1. Absence of Evidence

If upon arriving at a China Shop you discovered overturned tables, smashed porcelain statuettes, and general signs of mayhem, you'd nod understandingly when the shop owner told you that a bull had run through his China Shop. The evidence was clearly before you. However, if you arrived to find a pristine shop and were told that a bull had just run through, you'd likely raise an eyebrow. The fact that there is no notable damage to the shop is evidence that a bull did not run through it.

"In some circumstances it can be safely assumed that if a certain event had occurred, evidence of it could be discovered by qualified investigators. In such circumstances it is perfectly reasonable to take the absence of proof of its occurrence as positive proof of its non-occurrence." - Introduction to Logic, Copi, 1953, Page 95

Evidence comes in many shapes and sizes, from DNA in a tiny spot of blood to a hole in the wall where a car drove through, evidence is used to confirm something exists or occurred. A lack of evidence though doesn't necessarily disprove something; it just means there was not enough evidence to prove it. A suspected criminal may be acquitted due to a lack of evidence, even though he may in fact have committed the crime. So the absence of evidence does not mean there is evidence of absence. In other words, just because I don't have evidence, doesn't mean the thing didn't occur. It just means the evidence isn't there to prove that it did. But what if there should be evidence? Like our pristine China Shop, the absence of evidence that a bull had run through it is pretty reliable evidence that he in fact did not run through the China Shop.

The Biblical God of Abraham is an interventionist god. He didn't just create the Universe and leave; he was very involved in man's history on Earth. The Old Testament of the Bible is full of occasions of God's intervention in the affairs of man and the New Testament saw God actually father a son on Earth, who walked among man, lived with man, interacted with man, and died as a man. The accounts of God's activities are all preserved in the Bible.

What I propose to do is look for evidence where there should be evidence. If there were an absence of evidence, where there clearly should be evidence, shouldn't that cast doubt upon the veracity of that particular account in the Bible? Depending on the nature of the missing evidence, perhaps it should cast doubt on any other accounts by that particular author. If there were an absence of evidence on multiple Biblical accounts, creating doubt that these accounts are true, shouldn't it cast doubt upon the entire Bible as a true account of the history of God and his interaction with man on Earth? I'm going to look for big-ticket items; major events where God was clearly involved. Specific instances in the Bible where God was very clearly taking an active role with man on Earth, and where that role should have left evidence of his involvement, evidence that can be found through investigative means. If no evidence can be found to support the story of God's actions on Earth, where evidence should plainly exist, then that lack of evidence is evidence that the story never took place. If the story never took place, and this story featured God's actions specifically, then God's actions never took place. If God's actions never took place, and these Biblical tales are our only source of knowledge about God, then I propose the Biblical God does not exist due to a lack of evidence *where evidence should exist.*

Now you may argue that just because one of the Bible's tales about God's specific actions on Earth was not true, that is not evidence that God doesn't exist. I'll agree with that statement, however, what if none of the tales where God took action on Earth are true? If every account of God's involvement in the lives of mankind is found to be fictitious, and the Bible is the source for our knowledge of God, then I propose ladies and gentlemen that beyond any reasonable doubt, this being does not actually exist, but is a literary figure, a myth.

If you know your Bible history, you'll know there have been many translations of the original documents. In fact, we don't have the original manuscripts of the New Testament or the Old Testament. The earliest copy of the Old Testament is from the year 900. So we know we're working from copies of copies of copies, translated into many languages. But it's all that we have. Again, I assure you I'm not looking for errors in semantics or grammar to prove lack of evidence of God's activities. So we shouldn't have to engage in arguments over translation of the original Hebrew and whether the author meant to say that the Earth was shaped as a disc, a ball, or a sphere.

I hereby state that the absence of evidence, where there clearly should be evidence, should be considered evidence of absence. This is my premise, this is what I will set out to prove, and prove beyond a reasonable doubt. Without further adieu, let's go.

~~*~~

2. The Great Flood of Noah

In Genesis 1, God set about creating the Universe. While it is fairly clear that the authors mixed up the order of things, what with God creating Earth before the Sun and other stars, this is not the kind of thing I'm after. I'm looking for observable evidence on the Earth of God's activities, so we're not going to pick a fight over it, but it is clear that the authors did not receive Divine telepathic information about the formation of the Universe.

"In the beginning God created the heavens and the earth. The earth was without form, and void; and darkness was on the face of the deep. And the Spirit of God was hovering over the face of the waters. Then God said, "Let there be light"; and there was light. And God saw the light, that it was good; and God divided the light from the darkness. God called the light Day, and the darkness He called Night. So the evening and the morning were the first day."

"Then God said, "Let there be lights in the firmament of the heavens to divide the day from the night; and let them be for signs and seasons, and for days and years; and let them be for lights in the firmament of the heavens to give light on the earth"; and it was so. Then God made two great lights: the greater light to rule the day, and the lesser light to rule the night. He made the stars also. God set them in the firmament of the heavens to give light on the earth, and to rule over the day and over the night, and to divide the light from the darkness. And God saw that it was good. So the evening and the morning were the fourth day."

So as you can see, the author(s) of Genesis indicate that God made Earth the First Day, but didn't make the Sun and other stars until the Fourth Day. We know scientifically and logically that this isn't accurate, but again, that's not evidence of the absence of God's involvement in making the Universe, that's just evidence that the author(s) got it wrong and as previously stated, clearly didn't receive Divine revelation.

As we move through Genesis, a lineage of early man is laid out, with people living rather long lives of 800, 900 years and more. Then we get to Noah and the Flood, and this will be my first stop to search for evidence. God is directly involved with man on Earth in this tale, having decided that mankind was wicked and regretting ever creating us, He seeks out Noah.

And God said to Noah, *"The end of all flesh has come before Me, for the earth is filled with violence through them; and behold, I will destroy them with the earth. Make yourself an ark of gopherwood; make rooms in the ark, and cover it inside and outside with pitch. And this is how you shall make it: The length of the ark shall be three hundred cubits, its width fifty cubits, and its height thirty cubits. You shall make a window for the ark, and you shall finish it to a cubit from above; and set the door of the ark in its side. You shall make it with lower, second, and third decks. And behold, I Myself am bringing floodwaters on the earth, to destroy from under heaven all flesh in which is the breath of life; everything that is on the earth shall die. But I will establish My covenant with you; and you shall go into the ark — you, your sons, your wife, and your sons' wives with you. And of every living thing of all flesh you shall bring two of every sort into the ark, to keep them alive with you; they shall be male and female. Of the birds after their kind, of animals after their kind, and of every creeping thing of the earth after its kind, two of every kind will come to you to keep them alive. And you shall take for yourself of all food that is eaten, and you shall gather it to yourself; and it shall be food for you and for them."*

I think we can all agree that this is very specific, very direct involvement by God on the Earth and in the lives of mankind. The Bible is then very specific that everything that lived and breathed on Earth was drowned in a flood that lasted 150 days and covered even the highest mountains. God literally killed every living thing on Earth in one massive homicidal rage.

Now a mass extinction of this magnitude is sure to leave some evidence. We have had 5 major Mass Extinction events on the planet in the last 540 million years (a Mass Extinction Event means that at least 50% of all living species died) and we know this through the fossil record. Sadly, we're in the midst of a major extinction event right now, but no one pays much attention. That's a topic for another book though. So a massive calamity such as the Great Flood, where God Himself killed every living thing on Earth is sure to have left a massive fossil footprint. The Great Flood's mass extinction event will be easy to identify because the fossils will be modern humans and modern species of animals. We'll be able to find human fossilized remains by at least the tens of thousands, if not hundreds of thousands, mixed in with the fossilized remains of horses, zebras, lions, tigers, elephants, wolves, giraffe, and every other living creature at that time. And those fossils will be found everywhere on Earth and buried at the same geological level of rock and dirt since the flood occurred in a 150 day period in relatively recent history.

The two most commonly used dates for the Creation are 4000 BCE and 5500 BCE and the Great Flood took place somewhere between 3,000 and 4,000 years ago, with Archbishop Ussher indicating it was precisely 2348 BCE based on his calculations of the Bible's lineages and other dates. So archaeologists and geologists should find the fossilized evidence of the flood at those levels of rock and sediment. Geologists tell us we would find a similar layer throughout the world covered with pebbles, sludge, boulders, and other elements. However this layer of 3,000 or 4,000 year-old sediment has never been found. Neither have the layer of fossils, with all the different animal species that would be occupying those layers. We also have not found any of the fossilized remains of human beings buried in 3,000 or 4,000 year-old sediment.

So what does the evidence show us regarding the Great Flood of Noah that killed every living thing on Earth approximately 4,000 years ago? That it didn't take place. If we're willing to look at the evidence, the actual physical evidence that is observable and testable, we know that this flood did not happen. According to Genesis, God Himself specifically flooded the Earth to kill every man, woman, child and living and breathing thing except Noah and 7 other humans, and two of each animal on Earth. I believe I have effectively cast reasonable doubt upon the veracity of this story because there is an absence of evidence where there clearly should be evidence. This absence of evidence then, is evidence that this Biblical tale did not actually occur, so clearly God's involvement in the tale did not occur either.

As mentioned earlier in the book, the Catholic Church has come a long way from branding Galileo a heretic because he said that the Earth orbited around the Sun. The hierarchy of the Catholic Church has put in writing in their teaching documents that parts of the Bible aren't true. They're telling their millions of followers that they should not expect total accuracy from the Bible. I believe I'll be able to show at the end of our journey that the Church is correct, however only partially so. I believe I'll be able to show that much of the Bible is inaccurate and some is pure fiction and fantasy. But before we've even left the First Book of the Bible, before we've barely scratched the surface, we've seen that one of the most famous tales in human history, the Great Flood of Noah, did not occur and that one of the oldest Christian Church's in the world has basically stated so plainly and in writing. The evidence already shows us that the Bible is not the inerrant and infallible Word of God, and it's not just me saying it, the Catholic Church says it too.

~~*~~

3. The twin cities of Sodom and Gomorrah

In Genesis 17 we find the Lord speaking with Abram, who was 99 years old at the time. God decided he would now be named Abraham and that he would be the father of many nations. God establishes an eternal covenant with Abraham that involves the cutting of the flesh. This is where the Lord decides that every male child must be circumcised at 8 days old, whether he is born into the house of Abraham or *"bought with money from any foreigner who is not your descendant."* God goes on to state that He is going to have Abraham's wife Sarah (previously known as Sar'ai until God changes her name), who is 90 years old, give Abraham a son. He wants to establish a covenant with him too. So Abraham did what God told him, including having himself circumcised at age 99.

Moving on from this interesting tale of deal making, we get to the next stop in our investigation. A Biblical tale where the Lord God is directly involved in the lives of human beings and not just in conversation, as He was with Abraham, where there would be no evidence other than Abraham's word. In this tale, there would certainly be evidence of God's involvement. This is the story of Sodom and Gomorrah.

The Lord, along with a couple of His angels, dropped by Abraham's place for a visit and quickly, Abraham had Sarah whip up some food for them. As they ate, they chatted a bit about Sarah's future son, and then they began walking toward Sodom. Abraham tagged along.

What's interesting about the conversation that follows is that God dispatches His angels down to Sodom and Gomorrah to see if the evil and wicked ways of the people there that have reached His ears are true. Abraham then asks God if He would not spare the cities if there were any number of righteous people there. Why would God, who is both omnipotent and omniscient, need to confirm anything? He'd not only know whether there was wickedness in Sodom, He'd have known it before there ever was a Sodom. He'd also know if there were any righteous people there. It's the nature of omniscience; He knows everything past, present and future.

The angels stay at Lot's place in Sodom and he makes them a nice feast. But the town folk, aware of strangers in their midst, go to Lot's and demand that he bring out these strangers that they may know them. Lot, desperate to keep the angels from seeing the town's wickedness, offers up his virginal daughters to the town folks instead, so that they may do with them as they will:

So Lot went out to them through the doorway, shut the door behind him, and said, "Please, my brethren, do not do so wickedly! See now, I have two daughters who have not known a man; please, let me bring them out to you, and you may do to them as you wish; only do nothing to these men, since this is the reason they have come under the shadow of my roof."

The angels then pull Lot back into the house, render the intrusive town folk blind, and tell Lot to get his wife and kids and get out of town, for they would destroy the city, as the *"Lord has sent us to destroy it."* Lot dawdled a bit, so the angels finally took him, his wife and their two daughters and brought them out of the city. They argue a bit about where Lot would go, and the angels eventually agree that he can go to a small town called Zo'ar. Then, God had at it and destroyed Sodom and Gomorrah with fire and brimstone.

"Then the LORD rained brimstone and fire on Sodom and Gomorrah, from the LORD out of the heavens. So He overthrew those cities, all the plain, all the inhabitants of the cities, and what grew on the ground."

One rather startling thing occurred, which barely warranted a sentence in the tale: Lot's wife made the fatal error of looking back at the cities as they were being consumed by fire and brimstone from the heavens and she was turned into a pillar of salt.

The first thing to look for in our search for evidence of the truth of this account is whether there are any contemporary writings that support that it took place. By contemporary, I mean written in real time when the event occurred. There are none. Next would be to look for archaeological evidence of the existence of these cities in the location and the time period indicated by the Biblical account. Archeologists have been searching for these cities for almost one hundred years. Most believe they must have been near the Dead Sea, and it is there where the search has concentrated.

Interestingly, the word Sodom is a derivative of a Hebrew word for scorched or burnt and Gomorrah is from the Hebrew 'amar', which is a heap, or a ruined heap. This at least makes one wonder if these cities were named when the story was being written, which as we'll see in a moment, was well after the alleged event.

A large-scale excavation project in the ancient city of Bab edh-Dhra has been searching for evidence of the destroyed cities of the Bible. Numeira, another city in the vicinity, and Jericho are the only walled settlements in the area from the approximate time period of Sodom and Gomorrah. Tombs, ancient pottery, and other evidence of civilization were found there. Much of the pottery was intact. In fact, at the levels of dirt and sediment that correspond to the early Bronze Age tombs, human remains, deep bowls, jars, jugs, shell bracelets, beads and some wooden objects were found. None bared the evidence of having been destroyed by fire. So not only have the decades of excavation found no evidence of the fiery destruction of a thriving metropolis, but there is also no sulfur, which was known in Biblical times as brimstone.

Sulfur is found mostly near volcanic regions and has a yellow hue. Large deposits of sulfur can be found in Chile, Indonesia and Japan. It is a naturally occurring element that has many uses in modern civilization. It is not difficult to spot visually.

So what can we deduce from the evidence, or lack thereof, as to the truth of the Biblical account of God's destruction of Sodom and Gomorrah? The Bible tells us that these cities existed and describe where they were located. God, having consulted with His angelic scouts and determining the wickedness there to be unacceptable, rained fire and brimstone from the heavens and destroyed all who lived there, all the plain, and what grew on the ground.

There is no written evidence from a contemporary source that this occurred. The Bible dates the destruction of these cities to around 1712 BCE and the oldest texts of the Old Testament are the twenty-four fragments found among the Dead Sea Scrolls, dating from between 150 BCE and 70 CE. Biblical scholars have dated the likely composition of the Old Testament texts at 450 BCE. So the story of Sodom and Gomorrah was written over 1,000 years after it happened. Where did the author(s) of this tale in the Book of Genesis get his information? It was either completely fabricated by him, or it was a tale that had been passed along through oral tradition for hundreds of years. The names of the cities support that premise as they stem from words meaning scorched, burnt and ruined heap. It is also possible that God Himself revealed the tale to the author.

There is no way to know if God revealed anything to anyone. That is the nature of revelation; it's only shown to one person. As Thomas Paine wrote of Revelation in The Age of Reason *"it is revelation to the first person only, and hearsay to every other, and, consequently, they are not obliged to believe it."* I think by the end of this chapter I'll present enough evidence to suggest you should not believe that it was revealed since there is no evidence that it ever happened.

If God did indeed smote these thriving twin cities on the eastern bank of the Dead Sea with fire and brimstone, killing everyone in them and everything that grew there, there should be archaeological evidence of it. Scholars have used the descriptions of the Bible itself to try to locate the cities:

"And the border of the Canaanites was from Sidon as you go toward Gerar, as far as Gaza; then as you go toward Sodom, Gomorrah, Admah, and Zeboiim, as far as Lasha."

"And Lot lifted his eyes and saw all the plain of Jordan, that it was well watered everywhere (before the LORD destroyed Sodom and Gomorrah) like the garden of the LORD, like the land of Egypt as you go toward Zoar."

"Abram dwelt in the land of Canaan, and Lot dwelt in the cities of the plain and pitched his tent even as far as Sodom."

"And the king of Sodom, the king of Gomorrah, the king of Admah, the king of Zeboiim, and the king of Bela (that is, Zoar) went out and joined together in battle in the Valley of Siddim."

They have excavated these areas for decades and found evidence of civilization there, but no evidence of a large, thriving metropolis, and certainly no evidence for large-scale destruction by fire and brimstone. Brimstone, more commonly known as sulfur, is easily identified both visually and chemically. If sulfur had rained down from the heavens upon these cities on the Dead Sea, the level of sediment corresponding with the 1700 BCE era would be filled with it. It is not.

There is an absence of evidence that the Biblical cities destroyed by the God of the Bible ever existed, or that they were destroyed as described in Genesis, and there should be evidence if it were true. This absence then is evidence of absence. The fact that the account was written over 1,000 years after it allegedly took place, leads credence to the fact that it was nothing more than legend, or a completely fictional account to show the wrath of God and His distaste for wickedness. As in the tale of Noah's Flood, a classic tale of Biblical rage by God Himself never happened.

~~*~~

4. The Exodus

Disproving the existence of God is not a requirement for non-belief. On the contrary, proving the existence of God is what is required to eliminate the need for belief from the equation. If one believes things without evidence of their truth--or even of their existence--it is called faith, and sometimes, blind faith. As Arthur Clarke, famed author and inventor, stated so well: *"Science can destroy religion by ignoring it as well as by disproving its tenets. No one ever demonstrated, so far as I am aware, the non-existence of Zeus or Thor - but they have few followers now."* While I have never seen any compelling evidence of the existence of any gods, billions of people believe in one specific god and I have set out to disprove his existence. This is the god of Jews, Christians and Muslims who goes by the names Elohim, Adonai, Jehovah, Yahweh and Allah — and of course by the generic name of God.

To date, I have shown that the story of the Great Flood of Noah and the story of the ill-fated Sodom and Gomorrah never occurred. I selected these particular Biblical stories because God was directly involved. He specifically caused the Flood that killed every living thing on Earth save for the few human beings and their zoological cornucopia on the Ark. God specifically destroyed Sodom and Gomorrah Himself, with fire and brimstone. Neither of these tales is true as supported by the complete lack of evidence where there clearly should be evidence. For my next bit of investigative journalism, I will cover the epic tale of the Exodus of the Israelites from slavery and bondage in Egypt. This is perhaps the most well known tale of the Old Testament, celebrated each year by the Jewish people during Passover. Hollywood brought it to life with Charlton Heston playing the inimitable character of Moses, who wrought the power of God upon Pharaoh and the Egyptian people until finally, the Israelites were freed. He then led them to the foot of Mount Sinai where God himself carved the Ten Commandments into the face of the mountain. Surely this grand tale must be true! Think again Faithful Reader.

Exodus describes the Egyptian people forcing the children of Israel to work for them, building their cities for them. As the Israelites multiplied, the Egyptians grew more fearful of them as they thought they'd rise up and join the enemies of Egypt in a time of war. So the Egyptians made them *"serve with rigor. And they made their lives bitter with hard bondage – in mortar, in brick, and in all manner of service in the field. All their service in which they made them serve was with rigor."* In a particular show of fear, Pharaoh declared that all Hebrew male children must be tossed into the river. One Hebrew boy, being so beautiful that his mother couldn't cast him into the river, was put instead into a basket and floated down the river, where he was picked up by a daughter of Pharaoh and raised as if he were her own. She named him Moses.

Skipping along the Biblical narrative, we find that as an adult, Moses killed an Egyptian who was striking a Hebrew slave, and when Pharaoh found out about it, he wanted Moses killed, so Moses escaped, was found to be helpful to a local shepherd and received one of the shepherd's seven daughters for his troubles. But Moses would not be able to live happily ever after in the land of Midian with his new wife and son. Oh no, God had other plans for him. In Exodus 3, God explains his basic plan to Moses, while appearing to him as a burning bush. He indicates that Moses is to go to Egypt and tell the elders of Israel that God has seen their suffering at the hands of the Egyptians and will bring them out to the land of milk and honey. *"Then they will heed your voice; and you shall come, you and the elders of Israel, to the king of Egypt; and you shall say to him, 'The LORD God of the Hebrews has met with us; and now, please, let us go three days' journey into the wilderness, that we may sacrifice to the LORD our God.' But I am sure that the king of Egypt will not let you go, no, not even by a mighty hand. So I will stretch out My hand and strike Egypt with all My wonders which I will do in its midst; and after that he will let you go."*

I find it interesting that when God sets Moses upon this quest He intentionally hardens Pharaoh's heart repeatedly so that He may work more evils upon him and the people of Egypt. One by one, He inflicted plagues upon the land to show Pharaoh His power, yet each time He'd harden Pharaoh's heart so as to prevent the release of the Hebrew slaves. You would think God could pick one truly awesome display of supernatural power that would convince everyone of His existence and His might, but He felt it necessary to prolong the agony of both the Hebrew slaves and the plague-ridden Egyptians.

So God, through His messenger Moses and Moses' brother Aaron, brought blood to the Egyptians by turning the Nile and other water sources to blood. Pharaoh was not impressed. God then used His power to control our amphibian friends the frogs, and had the little critters hop all over Egypt, up into the beds of the people, even into their ovens. Lice were up next, followed by a swarm of flies and then a pestilence that killed all of the Egyptian livestock. Then God got personal and covered the Egyptians with boils on their skin.

God then had Moses bring a fiery hailstorm to Egypt that caused Pharaoh to say, "*I have sinned this time. The LORD is righteous, and my people and I are wicked. Entreat the LORD, that there may be no more mighty thundering and hail, for it is enough. I will let you go, and you shall stay no longer.*" But, when the storm ended, Pharaoh yet again hardened his heart and refused to let the Hebrews go. Locusts and darkness certainly weren't going to do the trick if all of the other plagues hadn't worked so it was time for the grand finale.

God decided He would kill the first born of every Egyptian, but not of the Hebrews. He gave Moses some very specific instructions on how to select, kill, cook and eat a lamb, including how to put its blood on door posts and such so that God would know not to kill anyone in a home that had blood on the door. He also told Moses that they were to celebrate this event for generations as a feast to Him. "*And it came to pass at midnight that the LORD struck all the firstborn in the land of Egypt, from the firstborn of Pharaoh who sat on his throne to the firstborn of the captive who was in the dungeon, and all the firstborn of livestock. So Pharaoh rose in the night, he, all his servants, and all the Egyptians; and there was a great cry in Egypt, for there was not a house where there was not one dead.*"

Finally, the children of Israel left Egypt. It was a massive exodus of humanity as 600,000 men, plus women, children and flocks and herds of livestock, all walked out of Egypt. But God wasn't done with Egypt yet for He still wanted to show His power and might and *"gain honor over Pharaoh and all his army."* So God hardened Pharaoh's heart yet again and had him pursue the Hebrews he had released from slavery.

As the Hebrews grew terrified that Moses had led them to a certain death in the wilderness at the hands of the Egyptians, God intervened and had Moses part the Red Sea so that the Hebrews could walk across on dry land. God held up the Egyptians with a pillar of cloud and darkness, then let them pursue through the parted Red Sea, although He knocked the chariot wheels off to slow them down.

"Then the LORD said to Moses, "Stretch out your hand over the sea, that the waters may come back upon the Egyptians, on their chariots, and on their horsemen." And Moses stretched out his hand over the sea; and when the morning appeared, the sea returned to its full depth, while the Egyptians were fleeing into it. So the LORD overthrew the Egyptians in the midst of the sea. Then the waters returned and covered the chariots, the horsemen, and all the army of Pharaoh that came into the sea after them. Not so much as one of them remained. But the children of Israel had walked on dry land in the midst of the sea, and the waters were a wall to them on their right hand and on their left.

So the LORD saved Israel that day out of the hand of the Egyptians, and Israel saw the Egyptians dead on the seashore. Thus Israel saw the great work which the LORD had done in Egypt; so the people feared the LORD, and believed the LORD and His servant Moses."

The Hebrews wandered around in the desert for forty years until they reached the foot of Mount Sinai. There, the story continues as God provides the Ten Commandments and so forth, but I think I'll pause here as we've got plenty to sink our investigative teeth into and look for the evidence to support this magnificent tale of freedom from oppression and slavery, handed to the Hebrew people by the God of the Bible Himself. There is no denying His direct involvement in this account and there should be scores of evidence confirming the tale. The Egyptians kept excellent records and one can only imagine the epic battle against the Hebrew's God, the plagues — particularly the one that killed every first born child in the country — and the ultimate death of Pharaoh and his armies in the Red Sea, which had miraculously opened for the Hebrews before closing upon the Egyptians, would be recorded. Of course there will also be the archeological evidence of the Hebrews long slavery in Egypt: "*Now the sojourn of the children of Israel who lived in Egypt was four hundred and thirty years.*" There will also be archeological evidence of masses of humanity — over 600,000 men alone, not including the numbers of women and children — living in the desert between Egypt and Mount Sinai for 40 years.

The reality is that there is no evidence that any of this epic tale of an enslaved people, rescued by God, ever took place. Biblical scholar Carol Redmount suggests people look at the story of Exodus as theology told as history, not as literal history. "*In the end, it was necessary that the theologically informed events of the Exodus epic relate to history, in the sense that a true historical heart to the narrative exist, but not that these events be bound by history. Particular, individual historical details were superfluous.*"

No evidence exists that a massive ethnic group departed from Egypt nor is there any evidence that the Sinai desert played host to over 600,000 people for decades. In fact, archeologists have been trying for over a century to find proof of the migration across the desert and have basically abandoned it. Israel Finkelstein, a Professor of Archaeology at the University of Tel Aviv and Neil Asher Silberman, editor for Archaeology Magazine, have written what is perhaps the most comprehensive analysis of this event and have concluded that not only did the Exodus not occur, but that the characters of Abraham and Moses likely never existed. At least, there is no evidence of their existence. They are mythical figures, legends in the account of the history of a people.

The biblical tale of the Exodus is nothing more than the written account of an oral tradition that was told for generations. It is the story of a people, an epic struggle against an oppressor and the freedom brought to them by God, who looked upon them with favor as He had made a covenant with the people of Israel. It builds ritual and ceremony atop tales of heroes that are still celebrated today, but the heavily embellished history of the Jewish people is not where my interests lie. Tradition and cultural history, whether real or imagined, is a part of the human story on Earth, as is the invention of gods.

~~*~~

There is no statute of limitations on murder, so let's imagine that God were on trial for the mass murder of every Egyptian first born, the Pharaoh of Egypt, and every member of his army. Additionally, He's been charged with the murder of every man, woman and child in the twin cities of Sodom and Gomorrah and many centuries before that, He is charged with the murder of every human being on Earth other than Noah and his family. If as a member of the jury, you were presented the evidence that I've just shown you in these cases, you'd have no choice but to acquit Him. There is not only no evidence to support that He committed these murderous acts, but in fact there is no evidence that there were any murders at all.

Now consider that the Bible and its stories are said to be the Word of God, divinely revealed to the authors of the various books. These three stories I have covered display God interacting on Earth with mankind and intervening directly in world events. But the evidence shows that these events are works of fiction, stories that have perhaps a bit more reality in them than Grimm's Fairy Tales. If you were asked, based on this evidence and this evidence alone, to state whether the being called God, Yahweh, or Allah was a real entity beyond a reasonable doubt, you could only state that He was not. There is not only no evidence that He exists, but the evidence that should be there to show His existence doesn't exist either.

Lastly, we should reflect on the many gods that man has worshipped, honored and paid homage to for countless generations. The Sumerian civilization, one of the oldest recorded civilizations in man's history, worshipped a pantheon of gods. The Egyptians had their pantheon of gods, as did the Incas, the Greeks, the Romans, the Nordic people, the Hindus, Aztecs, Mayans, the early African people, Native Americans and more. Reflect on all the reasons that you have for not believing in the existence of Thor, Odin, Zeus, Amlak, Jah, Aken, Poseidon, Inti, and Ra — just to name a few — and then apply those same reasons to the God of the Judeo/Christian/Islamic faiths. You don't need me to point out that those reasons send God to the same mythological place as Zeus.

~~*~~

6. The Wrap

Using both argument and physical evidence, I have provided what I think is sufficient evidence to establish reasonable doubt as to the existence of the Biblical God. In three specific occasions in the Old Testament where God took direct action on Earth, intervening in major world events that would have left evidence of His actions, the complete lack of evidence where evidence should exist indicates that these events are literary fiction, and as such, so is the main character, God. Moving God into the realm of other mythological gods allows us to have some healthy debate regarding Jesus Christ, whom Christians everywhere believe is the Son of God.

As I see it, we have a few basic choices regarding Jesus Christ:

1. He is a legend, like Abraham and Moses before him, completely fabricated by those who needed a central figure to build a new religion around.

2. He was an apocalyptic Jewish preacher who had convinced himself that he was the Son of God.

Since the Biblical God is not an actual entity but a literary character, obviously Jesus was not his actual son, so we are left to look logically at the evidence and make a decision based on an informed opinion.

There is no real historical evidence of the existence of Jesus. In other words, there is no archeological evidence, no contemporary written evidence about him (by contemporary I mean having been written during his lifetime), and no writings from the man himself. Nothing that we can point to and say, "this is evidence of Jesus Christ." Even though there were poets and scholars who were contemporary to Jesus, they failed to mention him in any of their writings. There are many writers from the first century who could have, should have, or probably should have mentioned Jesus Christ in their writings. In the Appendix, I provide information regarding these writers so you may judge for yourself how compelling it is that they were silent on the most important figure the world has ever known.

The first recorded mention of Jesus is in Paul's letters to the churches of Galatia. It is believed by scholars to have been written in the year 49, but the oldest copy in existence is from the year 200. Jewish scribe Josephus mentions him once in his writings from around the year 70, and of course there are the Gospels, both the canonical Gospels selected by the churches and the Gospels of Thomas and Mary. These were all written many decades after Jesus' death, and most historians feel that Matthew and Luke borrowed heavily from Mark, and others believe in a Q Document; a collection of sayings of a man that may have been Jesus Christ and served as the source for Matthew and Luke.

If you're a stickler for physical evidence, you can stop here because there is none and choose Option 1. Adding some additional strength to Jesus as literary character as opposed to actual historical figure are the inconsistencies in the Gospels. For example:

- Matthew and Luke both tell us that Jesus was born of a virgin, inseminated by the Holy Spirit. Mark and John make no mention of it.

- Matthew tells us that Jesus was already alive during the time of King Herod. Herod died in 4 BCE. Luke tells us that Jesus wasn't born until after Cyrenius became governor of Syria. Cyrenius became governor of Syria in 6 CE.

- Matthew describes the moment of Jesus' death on the cross leading to an earthquake, with tombs splitting open and dead men rising from their graves and going to visit people in the city. None of the others mention this.

- All four gospels have different versions of the resurrection: who was there, who saw Jesus first, how many angels were present, and whom Jesus spoke with after his resurrection from the dead.

With that kind of contradictory evidence, based on hearsay passed along for decades, any self-respecting judge would throw out the testimony from all four.

It is certainly possible that a Jewish preacher named Yeshu was roaming about Palestine in the first century with a small band of followers. It's also possible that the words attributed to him by the Gospels are truly his, and he had convinced himself that he was the son of the Jewish God Yahweh and was predicting the end of the world and the coming of God's kingdom. The search for the historical Jesus is a fascinating investigation, but it is beyond my scope with this book and ultimately, even if Yeshu existed, he could not be the son of Yahweh for Yahweh is a myth, and that is the reason I've written this book. Since God is mythical, the revelations Mohammad received in the desert were not divine in nature.

My sincere hope is that this book helps to shine a different light on old beliefs, and perhaps gets you to think a bit about what you may have been taught and why you believe it — if you do. We live in a time of technological wonders that allow us access to records, scientific papers, archaeological findings and more that made my little project possible. I am a truth seeker, someone who has learned over the years that there is an inordinate amount of misinformation that reaches our senses every day. There are answers out there to many of life's questions and mysteries. Questions and mysteries that once appeared magical have been answered and solved, one by one, and none of them ever turned out to be magic. Religion has its foothold in the world and tries to keep it by preserving the questions and the mysteries, by preventing the truth seekers from peering into their telescopes and their microscopes, from digging up the relics of the ancient world. The only way they can maintain that ability today is if we choose to allow it. They no longer have the power to intimidate, to imprison or to murder. We are free to examine life for the betterment of all, and as Socrates said "the unexamined life is not worth living."

~~*~~

Appendix

From "Rationality Eludes Us":

The most common cognitive biases that prevent you from being rational

- http://io9.com/5974468/the-most-common-cognitive-biases-that-prevent-you-from-being-rational

The Science behind why we don't believe Science

- http://www.motherjones.com/politics/2011/03/denial-science-chris-mooney

From "The Resurrection Myth":

Dan Barker's Easter Challenge

- http://ffrf.org/legacy/books/lfif/stone.php

From "Does evolution disprove Christianity?"

When humans faced extinction

- http://news.bbc.co.uk/2/hi/science/nature/2975862.stm

What does it mean to be human? Homo heidelbergensis

- http://humanorigins.si.edu/evidence/human-fossils/species/homo-heidelbergensis

Catholic Church no longer swears by the truth of the Bible

- http://www.bibleteachingnotes.com/templates/System/details.asp?id=29183&fetch=12882

From "The Power of Prayer":

Long awaited medical study question the Power of Prayer

- http://www.nytimes.com/2006/03/31/health/31pray.html?_r=4&pagewanted=all&

Francis Chan and John Piper get to the bottom of unanswered prayer

- http://www.christiantoday.com/article/francis.chan.and.john.piper.get.to.the.bottom.of.unanswered.prayer/27463.htm

Study of the Therapeutic Effects of Intercessory Prayer

- http://www.ncbi.nlm.nih.gov/m/pubmed/16569567/

From "The Great Flood of Noah":

Are the Biblical documents reliable?

- http://www.leaderu.com/orgs/probe/docs/bib-docu.html

Dynamics of origination and extinction in the marine fossil record

- http://www.ncbi.nlm.nih.gov/pmc/articles/PMC2556405/?tool=pmcentrez

Bishop Ussher Dates the World: 4004 BC

- http://www.lhup.edu/~dsimanek/ussher.htm

Problems with a Global Flood

- http://www.talkorigins.org/faqs/faq-noahs-ark.html#georecord

Was there really a Great Flood?

- http://www.theepochtimes.com/n2/science/great-flood-20470.html

Six Flood Arguments Creationists can't Answer

- http://www.lhup.edu/~dsimanek/6flood.htm

Deluge Geology

- http://www.asa3.org/ASA/PSCF/1950/JASA3-50Kulp.html

From "The twin cities of Sodom and Gomorrah":

The Kings of Canaan

- http://www.mazzaroth.com/ChapterFour/KingsOfCanaan.htm

Expedition to the Dead Sea Plain

- http://www3.nd.edu/~mchesson/edsp_beddescription.html

From "The Exodus":

The Oxford History of the Biblical World

- http://goo.gl/AVRdiO

Who were the early Israelites and where did they come from?

- http://goo.gl/S7Irhw

The Bible Unearthed

- By Israel Finkelstein and Neil Asher Silberman Free Press | 400 pages | ISBN 9780684869131 | June 2002

From "The Wrap:"

List of early writers who could have mentioned Jesus

- http://www.abovetopsecret.com/forum/thread118797/pg1

~~*~~

About the author

John Espinoza started out wanting to be a baseball player, but that dream died a quick and merciless death due to subpar skills. After giving up on his next dream of being a rock star, he worked as a musician for a short time and then tried other things like soldiering and being a helicopter pilot. He worked in the corporate world for 20 years and has contributed his DNA to four offspring. He likes lifting weights and is currently contemplating becoming a man about town.

His second book is A Collection of Musings: On Knowledge, Life, Love & Poetry, available at CreateSpace, Amazon and fine retailers everywhere.

# # #

Made in the USA
San Bernardino, CA
28 October 2017